FROM ROOFTOP TO
BASEMENT
DAMP DEFEATED

FROM ROOF-TOP TO BASEMENT
DAMP DEFEATED
SYMPTOMS · CAUSES · CURES

E.L. NICOLL · TREVOR PEEK

Quiller Press

Designed and produced by Strawberry Hill Press Ltd
24 Walpole Road, Twickenham, Middx TW2 5SN
in association with BP Aquaseal Ltd
Kingsnorth, Hoo, Rochester, Kent ME3 9ND
© BP Aquaseal Ltd
First published in 1982 by
Quiller Press Ltd, 11a Albemarle St, London W1X 3HE
ISBN 0 907621 09 0
Printed in Great Britain by
A Wheaton and Company Ltd Hennock Rd, Exeter EX2 8RP

Contents

Introduction

Caius Cornelius Tacitus, Roman historian (120–55 BC), had this to say of the Britons, and the land in which they lived:

"their sky is obscured by continual rain and cloud" and, "the soil will yield all ordinary produce in plenty. It ripens slowly but grows rapidly, the cause in each case being excessive moisture of soil and atmosphere".

That same 'excessive moisture' experienced some two thousand years ago by some luckless Roman tourist to these shores, could be said to have provoked the printing of the pages that follow.

For as rain and dampness cause excessive damage and deterioration to property – and often to the health of the dwellers therein – reliable ways and means of dealing economically and efficiently with damp, must always be welcome.

Hence it is hoped that this book will encourage and enable even the least talented do-it-yourselfer to cope with most damp problems, to save money and in the process to find much satisfaction in so doing. And if a task looks too daunting a study of what is necessary to put things right, as outlined here, will provide a better briefing for the builder, and a knowledgeable check on work done.

Products vary in their application needs and covering capacities, and instructions given in this book are but a good guide. The actual purchase should contain full details; study these before use, or indeed, before buying.

To successful damp-proofing . . .

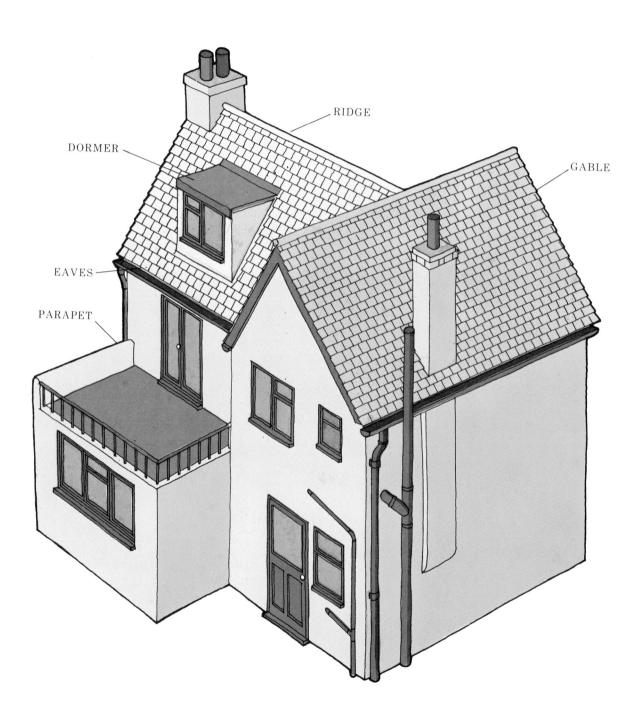

RIDGE

DORMER

GABLE

EAVES

PARAPET

Chapter One

Chimney Stacks

Let's start at the highest point of the house – the chimney stack which can deteriorate quicker than one would wish. It is the part of the building most exposed to weather, is built of varied materials which expand and contract at different rates with temperature or moisture changes, and of course is subject to heat and chemical action from flue gases.

Dampness can manifest itself in one of two ways. Firstly, when it is associated with rainfall. Secondly, when conditions are very humid, such as in misty and muggy weather when there is high humidity in rooms adjacent to the chimney.

Before attempting any repairs or damp-proofing to the chimney, flue or surroundings, a little detective work, or at least observation is advised so that time and money will not be wasted in taking wrong remedial measures.

Damp associated with Rainfall

Symptoms Almost invariably, if rain penetration is the cause of dampness, the dampness will appear as a patch on the surface of the chimney breast, or adjacent wall or ceiling, varying in intensity dependent on the amount and time span of rainfall, and may disappear during spells of dry weather.

Cause The most likely cause is due to the absence of, or a defect in, the damp-proof tray, metal flashing or cement fillet in the chimney stack or brickwork or other construction materials, which have become exceptionally porous or broken, allowing rain to penetrate.

Remedies Inspect the flashing, pointing and whole construction carefully in order to determine if and where failure has occurred. It may be visible from ground level, either with the naked eye or through field glasses.

Whatever has to be done, here are a few hints on how to go about it:

Flashings Traditionally flashings are constructed from metal chased into the brickwork along the upper edge, and dressed down to carry water away from vulnerable areas of construction. If faulty, these can be replaced to the original specification or by using a proprietary self-adhesive flashing. Some older properties have cement flashings which are prone to failure.

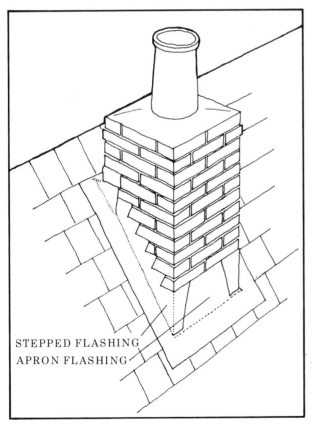

STEPPED FLASHING
APRON FLASHING

Typical chimney stack design

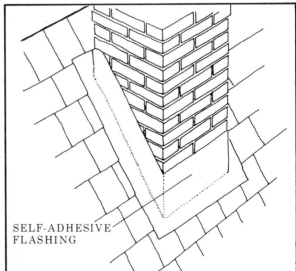

SELF-ADHESIVE FLASHING

Simple repair using self-adhesive flashing

To replace, remove flashings and thoroughly clean the surface. Cut new flashing to the length required, remove the release paper from the adhesive side, and press the bitumen adhesive layer onto the surface. Smooth into place using a flat trowel or some other means suited to the contour of the surface. When the flashing has to be joined, make an overlap of at least 25 mm (1″) so that upper sections go over lower sections.

Make sure no air blisters remain and all corners and contours are pressed firmly down. Where possible the upper edge should be chased into the brickwork, which can then be re-pointed with an appropriate mortar mix.

Brickwork Mortar joints of chimneys and some types of brick, may age rapidly due to their exposed position, allowing moisture to penetrate the stack, causing it to become unstable and dangerous.

Providing the chimney is structurally sound, an effective cure may be made by re-pointing defective mortar joints and cracked brickwork, or repair of renderings. Then apply over the whole brick area a silicone water repellent (for application notes see chapter 3 page 30). This will limit further deterioration for several years, and waterproof the surface without altering its appearance or colouring.

In severe cases chemicals from flue gases may have been absorbed into the building materials, having an adverse affect on the mortar, causing it to swell and crumble away. Here, the application of a water repellent may only provide a partial cure, the treatment having to be repeated as often as is necessary.

If the chimney is extensively perished or the stack distorted into a dangerous condition it should be dismantled and rebuilt, incorporating new flue linings where possible, which prevent the re-occurrence of flue gases being absorbed.

Damp-proof Tray If inspection of the chimney fails to identify the cause of the problem, but dampness persists in appearing during or shortly after rainfall, it may be as a result of a faulty or even non-existent damp-proof tray at the base of the stack.

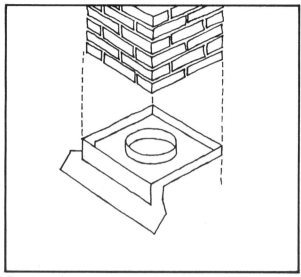

Damp-proof tray

This is not an easy fault to identify as the tray is buried within the structure, nor is it easy to cure, as it necessitates dismantling the stack, laying a new damp-proof course, and rebuilding. This is generally not a do-it-yourself job – scaffolding will most likely be needed for example – and quotations should be sought from local builders for the work to be assessed.

Damp not associated with Rainfall

Symptoms Damp might appear anywhere on a wall in the vicinity of the flue, not of necessity after rain, but when the humidity or water vapour content in the air is high. The patches of damp generally appear where there is a bend or a ledge in the flue, although it is not always easy to see or discover exactly where these features are. This dampness usually appears in older properties, and is often associated with a discolouration on walls or decorations.

Cause The dampness is generally due to salts in the brickwork and plaster, brought about by the condensation of flue gases and soot deposited within the chimney. When the humidity of the air in the room is high, these salts absorb moisture from the atmosphere to the extent that damp and stains appear, ruining wallpaper and other decorative coverings.

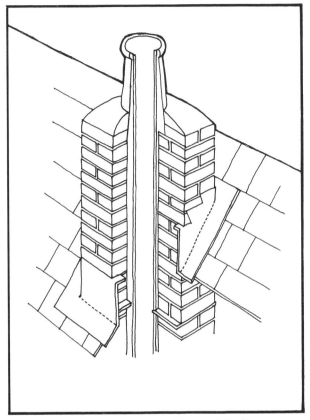

The chimneys defence system – flashings and flue liners

Remedies Current construction techniques now require the installation of effective flue liners to prevent these harmful compounds being carried into the building structure. Flue liners are more important with the use of closed heating systems using solid fuel, gas or oil-fired boilers, where air flow is restricted, thus increasing the chances of internal condensation. If the problem occurs with a chimney where linings are installed, a builder should be consulted to correct any defects in the flue lining.

In older properties where salt impregnation of the brickwork has continued over many years, the installation of a flue lining alone may not overcome the problem. A flue lining will prevent further contamination of the brickwork, but the salts already present in the structure will be a constant source of trouble.

A simpler and more economic course of action may be to provide a physical barrier on the internal surface of the wall, and varying courses of action are available.

The most effective is to remove the contaminated plaster and install a bitumen/latex barrier before re-plastering, ensuring that the treatment overlaps the affected area by 150–200 mm (6″ to 8″). (Application details chapter 4 page 34).

Foil-backed plasterboard can also be utilized to form a barrier.

Surface treatments can be applied to overcome the problems of re-plastering, by using for example, waterproof laminate and foils (see page 37 for details), or an aluminium sealer primer. These, however, may be prone to damage when re-decorating, when the treatment may have to be removed and fresh treatment applied.

Blocked Chimneys The chimney may be blocked by a nest, dead bird or fallen masonry. It has been known for a chimney to be deliberately sealed – when changing over from an open fire to central heating for example – in order to stop the rain penetrating down an unused flue, in the mistaken idea that this will stop damp.

Flues not in use should never be completely sealed. A small amount of ventilation must be provided by some means of an opening at the top and bottom of the flue.

Chapter Two

Roofs

Because they are out of reach and close inspection is not easy, roofs are rarely examined until trouble arises. Yet roofs with their greater exposure to the elements, should warrant regular inspection to ensure that they will keep out rain and snow.

Problems occur largely through a roof being constructed of different materials – slate, tiles, timber, brick, cement – all of which expand and contract at different rates in varying temperatures and moisture conditions. These differential expansion rates can cause cracks, splits and movement in the roofing materials, which eventually lead to the ingress of water.

If not promptly attended to, a leaking roof may be the cause of rapid deterioration of other sections of the structure – decay in timbers, damage to internal plastered surfaces, and possibly to decorations and household contents.

It is not always easy to trace the source of a leak in a roof. For example, a damp patch on a ceiling may be the result of water entering the structure some distance away from the visible signs of damp; water inside the roof space may run along timbers making diagnosis difficult.

It is therefore essential that some time is spent investigating the real cause of a problem to ensure that the source of any trouble is ascertained, and that appropriate roof repairs can be planned and carried out efficiently and economically.

The blame for a failure in the waterproof covering of a roof is often wrongly identified, and therefore care should be taken in inspecting flashings, copings and ridge, hip and valley tiles, all of which can be dealt with simply, without the necessity of covering or re-roofing the whole structure.

A wide variety of roofing materials are in common use. The design of the roof and choice of materials at the time of construction, is dependent on cost, availability and appearance, together with the required performance necessary for the type of building.

So lets go through the various materials of different types of roof surfaces, to find out where they may fail, and find a remedy.

Pitched Roofs

Natural Slate In the eighteen hundreds and early this century, slates were used extensively for roofing. Their durability has been proven because many of these roofs are in excellent condition today. Slates are still used, but due to their high cost are now mainly used for prestige buildings.

After prolonged weathering however, troubles could begin. Slates may become delaminated, worn, porous or cracked. Wind and thermal movement can cause the slates to move or lift. Fixing nails, holding the slates in position, become 'tired' or 'sick' due to corrosion, and break, allowing the slates to slip. Many older slate roofs were constructed without boarding or sarking felts, and any defects in the slating then allows water or snow to freely enter the loft space.

Inspection of a suspect roof can often be carried out from inside the loft; light will readily be seen to penetrate where slates are damaged or missing. With the loft light on or with a good torch, inspect the roof timbers for signs of water stains.

While inside the loft space it is an ideal time to inspect the roof timbers and rafters for decay and insect attack (see chapter 9 page 51).

Next inspect the external surface of the roof; pay particular attention to defects in the valley, ridge, or the eaves, ensuring that mortar fillets and joints have not cracked or fallen away. If sarking felt is incorporated in the design, make sure it carries water over any fascia and preferably into gutters, and does not shed water on to walls.

If only one or two slates have become misplaced then the remedy is simple, replace the slates. This can be done easily, but it is impossible to reach the original fixing. A hook made from aluminium, copper or lead, fixed to the exposed batten, the other end holding the lower edge of the slate, will provide adequate support (see diagram below).

Unfortunately, new slates have been and are still difficult to come by; secondhand slates can be obtained from demolition sites, but when broken slates are replaced with undersize or badly cut substitutes, leaks may occur. When confronted with this situation

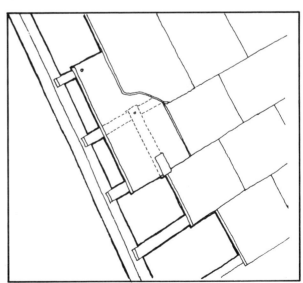

A hook fixing, for supporting replacement slate

Slate roof – in poor condition

or when the slates or fixings have generally deteriorated over the whole of the roof, allowing leaks in various places, the time has arrived to consider re-roofing, or covering the existing slates with a waterproofing treatment.

Uneven roof surface – roofing timbers too weak

Re-roofing is a specialist job, partly because it is unlikely that replacement will be of a weight identical with the old slating. In the majority of cases old slates are replaced with new concrete tiles, which may be heavier; if the load on the roofing timbers is increased, the structure may be unable to cope with the increased weight and excessive deflection of the roof support can occur, or, in rare cases, an outward movement of the upper portions of the walls could take place.

It is very practical therefore, to consider the application of a waterproofing treatment to the exterior surface of the existing roof, which can be applied by any householder who doesn't mind working on a rooftop. Various systems are available, the most widely used being a bituminous membrane treatment, which is simply applied by brush or soft broom. The method has many advantages.

The existing slates stay where they are, so that the roof is not open to the skies at any time, and, as all applications merge one with another, work can proceed as time and inclination permits.

The final finish, too, is not very much different from the existing roof; the slate ridges are retained, and the colour and appearance look much the same as the original slate.

The materials needed are easy to apply, and the finished treatment gives a durable, overall jointless seal, impervious to all weathers. Many such systems still allow the roof to 'breathe', enabling water vapour to escape through the roof, thus avoiding the risk of encouraging internal condensation.

Application Before the application of any waterproofing compound to the roof, its surface must be thoroughly clean. If moss or lichen are present they must be removed and their spores killed with a fungicide, to prevent further growth.

Missing or badly cracked slates must be replaced, although minor cracks or holes can be repaired with a self-adhesive flashing tape.

Flashings around parapet walls or chimneys should be lifted clear of the roof surface, so that when the treatment is applied it can be continued under the flashings to ensure these areas are waterproof.

Liquid waterproofing treatments are normally applied by brush or soft broom. As the first coat is applied a reinforcing membrane, consisting of an open weave glass fibre, is

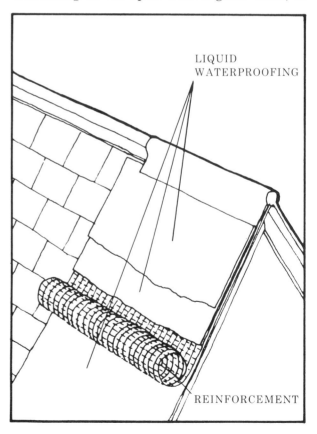

Weatherproofing, using a liquid waterproofing treatment

embedded from ridge to eaves into the wet film; this prevents the coating from cracking with any future movement of the slates. The reinforcement must closely follow the contours of the roof; but care must be taken not to stretch the fabric during installation.

Two further coats of the liquid waterproofing are then applied over the membrane, to produce a continuous and durable roof covering.

The ridge of the roof is usually treated after the slopes have been completed, applying the system in the same manner, but dressing the fabric over the apex of the roof and onto the slopes either side.

Once the treatment is fully dry, flashings which were lifted should be re-dressed onto the roof surface to complete the job.

There are a number of proprietary materials available to effect this type of repair, they can vary considerably in their make-up and application. Most are well proven and give very good durable service, but ensure that the material to be used comes from a reliable manufacturer.

If it is decided to employ a contractor to carry out the work, take great care to choose one with a reliable record. Most will give a performance guarantee, but this is of little use if the contractor cannot be contacted if problems arise. Beware of 'cowboy' contractors at all costs.

Spalling In and around the thirties some slates were imported from the continent and used fairly extensively. Unlike our native varieties, these slates contain impurities of calcium carbonate – chalk. In industrial atmospheres particularly, containing acid pollution, these impurities break down leading to delamination and spalling of the slate. The effect could be noticed over an entire roof or on a few isolated slates only. Slates so affected look unsightly and could eventually leak. There is unfortunately no 'cure' for this defect. Individual slates can be replaced but if the whole roof or large numbers of slates are affected total renewal of the roof will have to be made when the conditions so demand.

Tiled Roofs The majority of pitched roofs now constructed are clad with roofing tiles. Originally clay tiles were used; these tended to buckle slightly when fired in the manufacturing process giving them their rustic appearance. A relatively steep pitch to the roof was necessary to prevent rain penetration. The now prolific concrete tile overcomes this problem, most being designed with interlocking side-lap features and anti-capillary bottom laps.

Fixing is achieved by means of a 'nib' or projection at the upper edge of the tile, which is simply hooked over the battens. Clay tiles, particularly the older hand-made varieties relied on wooden pegs driven into holes in the tile to provide the nib. Pegs are obviously prone to decay, producing a situation similar to nail sickness in slates.

Water Penetration If water is entering a tiled roof it is normally the result of a defect in individual tiles, so in the case of a roof leak, look for a broken, slipped or missing tile and replace it. Overall treatment as described for slate roofs is rarely necessary, and it would be difficult to achieve a satisfactory result. The thickness of the tiles produces a deep step, a feature which is liable to weaken and break the continuity of a brushed-on liquid treatment.

Make certain also, particularly in the case of new property, that the eaves are properly constructed with a double-course of tiles,

Roof tiling

and also that the gable tiles are so formed with a slight fall away from the gable so that rainwater is diverted back from the edge.

Checks should also be carried out on valley, hip and ridge tiles, and flashings, as described for slate roofs, where similar problems may occur.

Spalling As with slates, clay tiles can show delamination or spalling of the top surface of the tile. Frost damage is generally the cause of the problem; if the whole roof surface becomes affected, complete replacement will be necessary. If single tiles are effected the cause may be due to underfiring during the manufacturing process. In this case it is unlikely that the whole batch will be defective and individual tiles can be replaced.

Spalling should not be confused with a general loss of the decorative granules from concrete tiles, which commonly occurs. This has no effect on the waterproofing qualities of the tile and should cause little concern to the homeowner, except that it means more frequent cleaning of gutters.

Sagging Sagging roofs are more common in older properties, where deflection of the roof structure may lead to leaks in the roof covering. It is possible that severe structural weakening of the roof timbers is the cause of the problem and these should be checked for insect or fungal decay and remedial treatment carried out (see chapter 9). If sagging occurs shortly after re-roofing, checks should be made on the loading and fixings of the roof timbers, as previously mentioned, if it is found that they cannot cope with the weight of the new roofing, professional advice should be sought, as it may be necessary to replace some timbers, or to provide additional support to the rafters with the provision of purlins and struts.

Cedar Shingles Western red cedar, used for the manufacture of roofing shingles, contains a natural preservative which at one time was thought sufficient to prevent fungal decay. This assumption was wrong, however, particularly with shingles used in areas of high humidity and rainfall; therefore all shingles intended for roofing are now treated with a suitable preservative.

Older shingles which have not been pre-treated in this manner, may show signs of

Example of a cedar shingle roof

fungal decay, indicated by a darkening in colour, and in extreme cases, by their becoming weak and porous.

If action is taken early, treatment with a wood preservative can stop or at least slow down the rate of deterioration – most wood preservative manufacturers have a grade specially designed for cedar wood application.

When decay has advanced to a stage where leaks are evident then re-roofing must be considered.

Sheet Materials

Asbestos-cement Flat or corrugated asbestos-cement is prone to cracking or to becoming porous. Also, although it may apparently not look porous, water and damp may be seeping through. Most of the asbestos roofs on domestic out-buildings are laid at too flat a pitch, encouraging water entry at side and bottom laps.

Cracking is often caused by fixings being too tight for movement; a 3 mm ($\frac{1}{8}''$) clearance between the fixing and the asbestos is advised. The clearance should be filled with a suitable mastic or a resilient cap under the head; either will accommodate any movement, yet stop water penetration.

Another cause of cracking, and this applies only to new asbestos-cement sheets, is the premature painting of one side, usually the top surface of the asbestos. This may cause bowing of the asbestos and a possible crack. New asbestos should be allowed to weather for at least six months before being painted or treated.

First-aid to visible cracks or splits can be given by the application of self-adhesive flashing or bitumen mastic, used as described on page 22.

A partially treated corrugated metal roof

Using a bitumen mastic to seal asbestos-cement sheeting

Overall treatment to overcome general porosity can be carried out, using a brush-applied liquid waterproofer. An alkali resistant product (such as bitumen or acrylic emulsion paints) should be used as the high cement-content of the sheets may adversely react with some paints.

The receiving surface must first be thoroughly cleaned, and if moss or lichen is present a fungicidal wash applied and allowed to dry; proprietary brands are available but a satisfactory substitute is household bleach, diluted with 15–20 parts water.

The surface of asbestos-cement sheeting may become 'soft' with exposure to weather and as the cement content of the sheets erodes away. It is therefore essential to use an appropriate primer to consolidate the surface and provide good adhesion for the waterproofing treatment; for example when using a bitumen emulsion waterproofer, a solvent based bitumen primer, or bitumen paint diluted with 20% white spirit should be applied, and allowed to dry.

Metal Roofs: Lead or Zinc These materials, because of their cost, are now but rarely used on new roofing, but may be found on older properties.

Where they do exist, rain penetration may be caused by one or a number of reasons. Through corrosion and weathering, lead and zinc may become pitted and therefore porous. Being metal, these materials expand and contract at a rate greater than that of most other materials, and unless laid in comparatively small areas, cause problems when they shrink and gaps appear. Large overlaps at joins are therefore necessary, but in time these may tear or lift, allowing water to penetrate.

Gaps and splits can be remedied, as previously mentioned, with a suitable mastic or self-adhesive flashing, and roof areas can be treated overall as described on page 22.

Galvanised Sheeting This material is affected in time by atmosphere and or bimetallic corrosion of both sheet and fixings. Bimetallic corrosion being the effect (adverse in this case) of one metal on another. Fixings should always be of the same metal as the sheeting.

Galvanised steel sheets suffer eventually from corrosion, particularly if and where sheets are cut or drilled, because here the galvanised protection is lost.

Galvanising is also weakened by washings from other metals, for example, from copper flashings.

Although it is imagined that most readers will have only a limited appetite for the subject, BRS digest No. 146 – Modern Plumbing Systems, contains a table showing corrosion risks with dissimilar metals. This digest can be obtained from H.M.S.O.

For protection, these types of roof surfaces should be coated with a bitumen paint approximately six months after installation, although an etching primer may be necessary to provide good adhesion of the paint.

Flat Roofs

Flat roofs are usually covered with asphalt, roofing felt, lead, zinc, iron or steel.

Although theoretically flat, they should, of whatever construction, be built with a slope or 'fall' to allow rain to run off into a gutter.

It is lack of sufficient fall, either because it was not built into the initial construction or due to subsequent movement of the roof, which often leads to 'ponding' on the roof surface.

If the roof surface remains watertight, the 'ponding' caused by insufficient fall does not necessarily create a damp problem, for the water thus collected may eventually evaporate. Despite this, ponding can eventually weaken some finishes, and the roof fall should be corrected.

Ponding can also occur because the drainage system, gutters and downpipes, may be blocked. This of course is easily ascertained and the blockage cleared.

However the different types of roof surfaces deteriorate for different reasons, so we will discuss them separately.

Asphalt There are a number of reasons why an asphalt roof may fail, although any of these failures may be easily remedied.

Asphalt suffers from blistering and cracking, and although this may not cause damp problems, regular inspection and treatment will prevent future trouble.

Blisters are produced by trapped moisture in the roof; they mainly appear during warm weather when the asphalt is relatively soft and any water below the asphalt is transformed into water vapour, with an associated increase in pressure.

It is unlikely that this moisture causing the problem has found its way into the structure due to a failure in the asphalt itself, but more likely because of moisture or rain trapped at the time the asphalt was laid.

Interstitial condensation (condensation within the building fabric) in the roof structure can produce the same or worse effect, especially in domestic properties where high volumes of water vapour are created in the room below; this permeates through the ceiling, and becomes trapped under, and to the detriment of, the roof covering.

To overcome interstitial condensation, a vapour barrier will have to be installed in the ceiling, and it may be necessary to also dry out the roof structure to provide a complete cure. Professional advice should be sought.

Blisters are unsightly, but unless they are the cause of water entering the building they are best left alone.

If leaks are apparent the asphalt should be gently softened with a blow-torch and the blisters cut open. The roof structure below should first be allowed to dry out and the blister flattened and re-sealed using a bitumen mastic, or a patch of self-adhesive flashing.

Cracking and crazing are usually caused by thermal movement, or construction faults associated with expansion joints, or shrinkage of the base on which the asphalt is laid. Particular areas subject to damage in this way are where asphalt has been laid over a joint in the roof slab, or where the roofing should join up with a parapet wall.

Any definite cracks can be filled with a bitumen mastic or covered with a strip of self-adhesive flashing. If the area is crazing then it may be best to consider an overall treatment of the entire roof (see page 22). If the problem is where the asphalt roof joins a parapet wall, then seal the joint with self-adhesive flashing.

After long exposure, and as asphalt ages, it may become porous in places, although it may not be possible to see any major faults. Replacing an asphalt roof is definitely work for a specialist firm, although an overall treatment to waterproof and protect the asphalt is easily carried out by the home owner. (See overall treatment page 22).

As many of the defects which occur in asphalt covered roofs are a result of movements of the roof or supporting structure, the severity of such problems can be reduced by ensuring that solar heat gain is kept to a minimum. Application of a coat of reflective chippings, or a bitumen-based-aluminium paint will moderate extremes of temperature which cause movement, and will also extend the life of the asphalt.

Felt Roofs These are mostly proprietary roofing materials made by impregnating and coating matted fibre with a bituminous material. Several grades, each grade designed for a specific purpose, are available in varied weights, strengths and surface finishes.

Although bitumen felt roofing can be found on sloping as well as flat roofs, the majority of felt used in domestic situations is on flat-roofed extensions, dormer roofs or garages. A built-up system is normally employed using three layers of felt, fixed with a hot-applied bitumen adhesive. Most flat roof areas are finished with a coating of reflective chippings, again fixed with a bitumen adhesive.

The main problems experienced with felted roofs are similar to those found in asphalt.

Blisters occur due to the presence of moisture trapped beneath the felt layers. As with asphalt, residual construction water or moisture vapour from the dwelling below could be the cause of the problem, but checks should be made on the laps of the felt to ensure that they are watertight.

It should be possible to establish whether a blister is filled with air or water by pressing lightly on it. If the blister appears to be filled with air and no leaks are apparent within the building, remedial action may not be necessary, but periodic checks should be carried out to ensure that the situation does not deteriorate.

Blisters which are causing leaks or are filled with water, and which will eventually seep into the property, should be treated as follows:

First remove the chippings, if any. Cut across the blister – in hot-cross bun style, and peel back the flaps. Dry the roof substrate, and stick the flaps back down with a cold-applied bitumen adhesive. It is advisable to then seal the cuts with a bitumen mastic or self-adhesive flashing, and which will ensure the repair is completely waterproof.

Splits are as simple to deal with; they are caused by excessive movement of the substrate which the felt cannot accommodate.

The adjacent area should be thoroughly cleaned of all foreign material and any chippings removed from the surface.

A strip of self-adhesive bitumen flashing can be stuck down over the split, easily and effectively sealing it.

Alternatively a length of felt cut to size, so that it overlaps the defect by approximately 50 mm (2″), is loose-laid over the imperfection. This should be covered by a further layer of felt 200 mm (8″) wider than the first, this being fully bonded to the roof surface and first strip

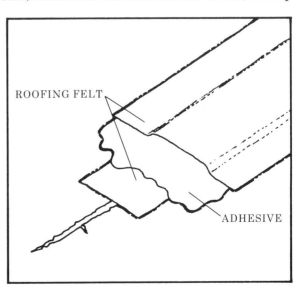

Repairing a crack, using felt to allow for any future roof movement

Application of a liquid bitumen based waterproofing treatment

using a bitumen adhesive (see diagram on page 19). This provides a joint which can accommodate any further movement in the roof slab without placing a strain on the roofing felt causing it to split.

In all cases where leaks in felt roofs occur it is advisable to consider using the above methods in conjunction with an overall waterproofing treatment (see page 22).

As with asphalt the felt will last longer, and the severity and occurrence of defects will be minimised if a solar reflective coating is utilised. Light coloured reflective chippings or a solar reflective bitumen-based aluminium paint should therefore be applied to all flat felted roofs.

Felt coverings to pitched roofs on domestic properties are normally restricted to timber roofed outbuildings, for example, garages and garden sheds. In these instances, only one layer of felt is generally used.

The felt should be held in place by large-headed clout nails. An adhesive should not be used for fixing direct to the timber, as the timber may swell and/or contract and split the felt.

If damp problems occur, check the overall condition of the felt. If in poor condition, do not despair, even re-covering with new felt is a relatively simple process.

Minor repairs to an existing roof can however be carried out, where necessary. Splits and tears can be patched using self-adhesive flashing of the appropriate width, cut to length and firmly stuck to the roof surface. Ensure that the edges of the repair are bedded firmly down so as not to allow water to enter.

Check areas where the felt overlaps, these should be sealed with an adhesive; if not, water may easily penetrate into the roof. If adequate overlap has been provided a cold applied bitumen felt adhesive can be used to seal the surface, prior to firmly nailing as detailed below.

Instruction for Fixing Old felt and fixings should be removed and the roof boards inspected to ensure they are sound and even. Re-nail loose boards, and replace any which appear defective.

Roofing felts should be laid from gable to gable, starting at the eaves and working upwards to the ridge. The roofing felt should be cut to length, allowing for an overlap of 40 mm (1¾") at each gable end and preferably left to flatten out before use.

The first sheet should be laid in position with bottom edge overlapping the eaves by 40 mm (1¾"). Fix the felt by nailing the large-headed galvanised clout nails at 600 mm (24") centres approximately 25 mm (1") in from the top edge of the sheet.

Carefully bend down edges of felt over gable end and eaves, nailing at 50 mm (2") centres. Finish corners neatly by folding felt underneath and nailing.

Apply the second and successive sheets in the same manner, once again allowing an overlap of 40 mm (1¾") at each gable end. An overlap of not less than 80 mm (3½") should be allowed over the lower sheet. Fix by nailing the top edge at 600 mm (24") centres.

Hold back the lower edge of the upper sheet, and coat all laps with a cold applied bitumen roofing-felt adhesive. Press the overlapping sheet back into position and nail at 40 mm (1¾") centres along the lap.

When both sides of the roof have been

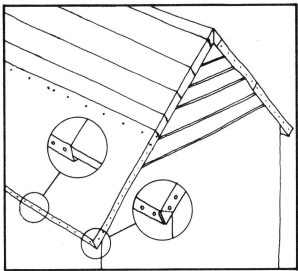

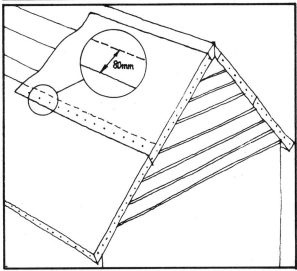

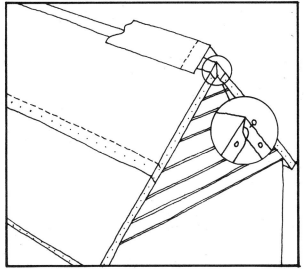

felted use a 300 mm (12″) wide strip of roofing felt for capping the ridge. Apply by bedding laps in a cold applied bitumen felt adhesive and nailing at 40 mm (1¾″) centres as previously detailed. Carefully fold the felt over the ridge and repeat on the other side. Finish by neatly folding edges overlapping the gable ends and nail into position.

Concrete Roofs Few domestic properties have concrete roofs, but there are exceptions.

Concrete in itself is not necessarily waterproof, and also may be prone to cracking. Cracks can be treated with the application of a self-adhesive flashing, or filled with a suitable flexible mastic. It is always preferable to apply a waterproof covering to concrete roofs and an ideal method is as detailed on page 22.

Dormer Roofs Dormer roofs warrant a special mention as their design can make diagnosing the cause of a leak particularly troublesome.

Basically, a dormer roof is a flat area protruding from a sloping one, and leaks can be caused by one or both roofs being at fault.

If a leak is discovered, first carefully check the joint where the flat roof meets the sloping roof. There might be a flashing along this joint, and the most common source of a leak in this area is because the flashing has been damaged or moved, and it no longer throws water away from the joint.

Method of fixing one layer of felt to a timber outbuilding roof   A dormer roof

The flat roof should also be carefully examined to ensure that it is sound and waterproof. Dormer roofs are usually covered with lead or roofing felt. Lead tends to pin-hole over the years and if not treated, such holes make perfect entry points for water. Roofing felts perish with age or become damaged allowing water to penetrate.

Reference for waterproofing should be made to the section dealing with the relevant type of roof surface.

Overall Treatment Without a doubt, except for putting right minor faults, the best way to deal with a deteriorating roof is to strip and replace it with new.

There are major snags to the ideal however. Specific skills are required to do the job. The cost is likely to be prohibitive. The time to carry out the work may be a handicap. And taking off a roof also means getting something replaced before rainfall!

A useful alternative to re-roofing may be to undertake remedial measures to correct leaks, and prevent further deterioration by applying a liquid waterproofing treatment to the existing roof.

Products are available from DIY shops and builders' merchants, suitable for application to most types of roof coverings; among the more frequently used are bitumen emulsions, which provide an effective seal for a leaking roof.

These materials are invariably sold ready for use and are applied to the roof by brush or broom. The surface to which they are applied must of course be thoroughly clean, any chippings on the roof must be removed together with any material which may affect the adhesion of the coating. Moss or lichen can effect the long term performance, and should be removed, using a fungicide solution to prevent early re-appearance.

Before carrying out an overall treatment, cracks and holes in the roofing material should be repaired – a non-setting bitumen mastic is often well suited for this. Larger cracks can be sealed by using the mastic in conjunction with metal cooking foil; sandwiching the foil between layers of mastic will produce a joint that will not open with movement of the crack and so ensure a lasting watertight seal.

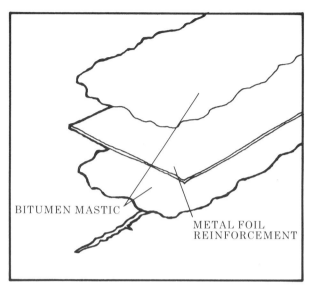

A simple crack repair, using bitumen mastic with a metal foil reinforcement

Once the preparation work is complete and porous surfaces, such as concrete or asbestos-cement are suitably primed, application of the coating can be carried out.

Normally a two-coat application is sufficient, but in severe cases when the roof is in very poor condition, the installation of a membrane, as described for slate roofs, is to be recommended (see page 14).

Once the treatment is completed a solar reflective coating of chippings or a suitable roof-finishing paint can be applied if desired.

Glass Roofs

Skylights, conservatories, and the greenhouse, so frequently begin to let in water along the wood or metal glazing bars. Even if new putty is applied, the bars may have warped and water soon penetrates.

Symptoms Defects are usually visible, for rain drips straight down into the landing or area below.

Remedy This is simple – seal over the top of the glazing bars – easily achieved by applying a waterproofing tape; this usually consisting of a base fabric impregnated and coated with a specially formulated waterproofing compound. It will withstand expansion and contraction, is durable, does not harden, adheres firmly and readily moulds to irregular surfaces.

Application The surface must be clean and

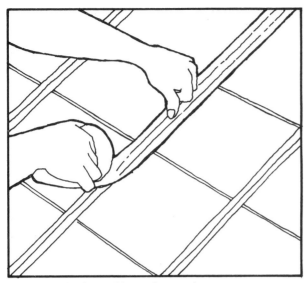

Sealing glazing bars with weatherproof tape

dry. Old wood should first be sealed with a coat of paint (either emulsion or oil-based).

Simply press the tape well down on to the surface to be weatherproofed, following the maker's instructions, and ensure all air is excluded. Smooth down centre of tape first then work outwards, along the length of tape.

The tape should overlap adjoining surfaces by a minimum of 6 mm ($\frac{1}{4}''$) each side.

Where panes of glass or roof sheets overlap, it is essential to prevent bridging of the tape over the gap. Cut the tape to allow for at least 25 mm (1″) overlap and commence a new run of the tape on the pane or sheet.

Where desired, normal paints can be applied over the tape, provided care is taken to allow the paint to flow on with the minimum of brushing.

The compound can be cleaned off glass by wiping with a rag dipped in paraffin or white spirit.

Application during exceptionally hot weather should, if possible, be avoided as softening of the waterproofing compound on the tape may make application difficult.

Parapet Walls

Parapet walls may present damp problems. In their original condition the coping and flashing details may well have been water-proofed, but as the building materials weather, they can become porous. Some movement may also take place, opening up joints and loosening the mortar.

Parapet walls should be built with a damp-course beneath the coping, but the damp-course may be non-existant or have perished, cracked or ruptured. The copings themselves should have a drip groove cut into the under-side, to prevent water tracking back on to the face of the wall.

The parapet should also be provided with a damp-proof course at or near the base of the wall, slightly above roof level and which should protrude on the external side to present a drip edge to carry water away from the building. On the internal face the damp-proof course should be extended by means of a flashing to discharge the water on to the roof surface.

Remedies Defects associated with a failure of the damp-proof course at the base of the parapet leave little alternative but to dis-

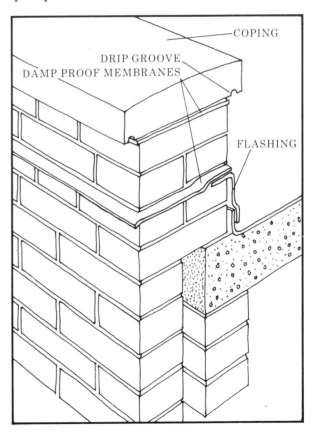

Section through parapet wall – illustrating damp-proof course detail

mantle the wall, lay a new damp-proof course and rebuild. However, closer inspection of the damp-proof course may provide an answer to the problem.

Ensure the damp-proof course protrudes on the external face to provide a drip edge; if missing a metal flashing, available from builders' merchants, can be installed directly under the damp-proof course to carry water away from the wall surface. On the internal side of the parapet, inspect the flashing, which should marry with the damp-proof course and be dressed over the roof covering. If the flashing is damaged or defective it should be replaced, using either conventional lead or self-adhesive bitumen-backed flashing.

The second problem area is at the top of the wall. First inspect the underside of the coping stones; the drip groove may have become damaged or filled with moss or dirt. Clean and make good where necessary. Ensure that the stones themselves are not loose and in a dangerous condition; if so they must be removed, and re-laid in fresh mortar. It is advisable when doing this to replace the damp-proof course on which the copings are laid.

If the copings are not loose ensure moisture is not penetrating through cracked or porous mortar joints; then re-point where necessary with a sand/cement mix (one of cement to three of sand). If water is penetrating inside it is also likely that the damp-proof course is damaged. Replacement may be advisable, but treatment with a waterproofing system incorporating a reinforcing membrane as described for slate roofs (page 14), applied over the top and sides of the coping will provide an effective substitute. The treatment should not continue under the lip of the coping as this will bridge the drip grooves and allow the water to run down the face of the wall.

Abutments

In this chapter an abutment refers to a roof which makes contact with a wall, the wall then extending upwards to form a further storey. Examples of this occur when an extension or enlargement to an existing property has been added, or where a garage is attached to the external house wall.

The abutment is a frequent source of damp penetration. Damp symptoms could appear anywhere below, for the roof usually slopes outward and downward, and water runs along the joists or rafters and drips off anywhere. Damp could also appear on one or both sides of the wall below.

The joint between the roof and wall may have developed a crack or the flashing which has been installed may have been damaged. These should be inspected, repaired or replaced. Using a bitumen mastic, fill all cracks and splits which may have opened. Repairs to flashings can be achieved by either reinstating the flashings or by using a self-adhesive bitumen flashing as previously described.

A cavity tray should be incorporated above any point where a roof joins a cavity wall; this will intercept any water that may penetrate through the external leaf of the wall, and which would otherwise run down into the building causing damp to appear lower in the structure. Cavity trays can be purchased preformed, though they are often formed in-situ from lead strips, felt or plastic sheeting. Care

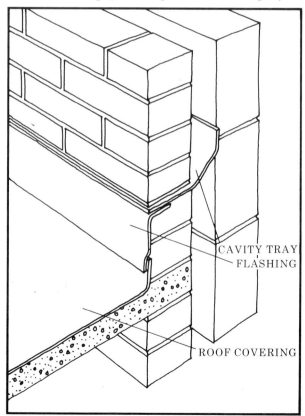

Abutment with cavity tray between inner and outer leaves of wall

must be taken when installing, as this requires bricks to be removed from the outer leaf of the wall, and advice on fixing should be sought from the manufacturers, otherwise a reputable builder should be contacted.

Gutters

Faulty or wrongly placed gutters are the cause of many damp problems. They are often not easy to reach and cope with, and for this reason are often ignored until real trouble starts.

Usually too, a builder's charge for putting right a gutter is out of proportion to the remedy involved. So a regular inspection is advised, with a determined attempt to deal with any problem oneself.

Box Gutters

Pitched roofs may be formed with an internal gutter between them, with a covering of metal sheeting or felt. These valley gutters are designed to carry water shed by the roofs to an outlet to which a downpipe is connected.

The box gutter is not built for foot traffic,

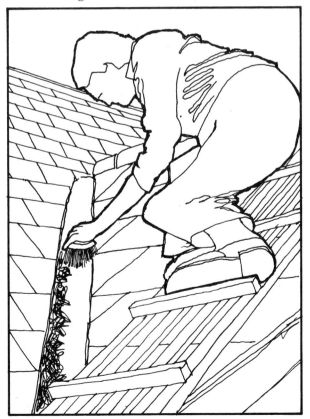

Cleaning a valley gutter

yet often workmen walk along them for example, when fixing a television aerial. This damages the structure, causing splits and cracks in the waterproofing sufficient to let rain through.

Box gutters are easily blocked with leaves and other debris, causing deep pools of water to accumulate, which seep through inadequate waterproof covering between roof ends and gutter.

Melting snow causes the same problem, especially when the sun shines on one section only of the gutter, so that melted snow is blocked by that unmelted.

Remedies The obvious first step is to completely clear the gutter of leaves, dirt, lichen and rubble, if any, so that the entire surface is clean and water runs away freely.

Make certain too, that the outlet and the downpipe are not blocked. By clearing away any blockage, the damp problem may be solved, or at least alleviated. If water penetration is still a problem, it is probably due to a defect in the gutter itself. Investigation should be undertaken to determine if the fault is restricted to a damaged section of gutter or if age has led to a general deterioration of the supporting decking or roof structure.

If the damage is limited to a hole or split, repair with a self-adhesive flashing. Choose a suitable width and cut a length so that the repair will overlap the imperfection by at least 50 mm (2″) all round. Thoroughly clean the adjacent surfaces and ensure they are as dry as possible before pressing the patch firmly into place.

If the damage to the gutter is more extensive, then an all-over treatment is to be advised. Individual areas which are in poor repair should be pre-treated as above; or with a bitumen mastic, with a metal foil reinforcement, as described on page 22.

A bitumen treatment incorporating a membrane can then be installed to provide an economical overall treatment to the gutter. Always ensure that all surfaces are thoroughly clean, and remember the treatment should continue over the entire gutter surface, and be taken up beneath the roof eaves.

Brush on a coat of bitumen emulsion and while it is still wet, bed in a reinforcing membrane of an open weave fibreglass cloth. Ensure that the membrane closely follows the contours of the gutter, and that there are no folds, creases or bulges to impede the flow of water. Where it is necessary to join two lengths of fabric, they should overlap by a minimum of 50 mm (2″). Overlap so that the end of the fabric on the 'flow' side is above that of the adjoining piece, so that there is no ridge to obstruct the flow of water. A further coat of emulsion should be applied to completely cover the reinforcing fabric, and then allow this treatment to dry. A third and final coat of emulsion should then be applied. The falls in a box gutter are rarely adequate and two final coats of emulsion should be of a heavy-duty nature to ensure they will cope with the severest conditions.

Guttering

Gutters round the house cause problems in a number of ways.

The supporting brackets may be placed, or have sagged, so that the fall is inadequate, non-existent or even in reverse. The collected water then flows over the side or out at the wrong end of the gutter.

Blockages occur with fallen leaves, nests and nest material. Joints leak, either through the jointing material rotting and falling out, or the bolt holes rusting open.

Along the length of the gutter, splits, cracks or holes may have occurred.

Inadequate rain outlets may be the cause of overflow, but this is rare, and should it seem apparent in a new building, the builder or surveyor should be consulted. When there is really prolonged torrential rain, most gutter systems seem inadequate! But this causes little, if any, damage, and is too infrequent to cause serious, long lasting damp penetration.

Damp Symptoms White patches may appear on the external surface of the wall, caused by excessive moisture bringing salts resident in the brickwork to the surface as efflorescence.

Damp patches may appear on the inside walls, and drips falling from faulty guttering may cause considerable inconvenience.

Remedies The first thing to look for is a blockage to clear – it may be all there is to do. Otherwise look for inadequate fall. Pour water in at what should be the higher end, and if the liquid doesn't run away, reset the brackets. This is not always easy as the screws will not turn and invariably only one hand can be used as the other is gripping the ladder. It is best done with the section of the gutter removed, having first marked how high the bracket is to be before re-setting.

Leaking joints in metal, concrete or asbestos-cement gutters can be treated by unscrewing the joints, trowelling a thick coat of bitumen mastic around the drop section of the gutter and re-bolt. Neatly point up the excess mastic squeezed out. This will give a flexible, watertight joint.

Plastic guttering is normally produced with push fit jointing systems, and if leaks occur with these, the cost involved in replacing with new seals or jointing sections is relatively low, and easy to carry out. Due to its high rate of thermal movement, the joints must allow for the plastic to expand and contract.

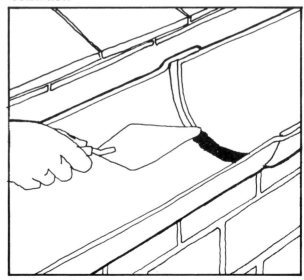

Removing excess bitumen mastic from guttering after re-sealing joint

Concrete or asbestos-cement guttering may in time become completely porous, in this case, leaks will be difficult to trace as they will not be associated with a visible fault. To overcome this problem the internal surfaces should be thoroughly cleaned, primed and treated with one or two coats of a bitumen waterproofer.

Rainwater Pipes

The most common cause of an overflowing downpipe is through blockage of leaves, tile grit, moss and algae deposits and other debris.

Older pipes occasionally split, particularly at the back where, possibly because being close to the wall, paint isn't put on very thickly, if at all, and rust eats through.

Fixings fail or move, throwing the pipe out of line, so that rainwater runs out of the top or any one section.

Damp Symptoms Fortunately, an overflowing or leaking rainwater pipe is easy to see, and therefore, the cause is likely to be discovered before a serious damp situation occurs.

However, if neglected for long, it is likely that the outside wall taking the flow of excessive water will develop a white efflorescence deposit, which will spoil the appearance of a wall.

If the wall is solid, damp stains may appear inside, adjacent to or anywhere below the level of the overflow. Even a cavity wall could be bridged by moisture travelling across mortar or a brick lodged between the outer and inner wall.

Remedies Blockages tend to occur at the gutter outlet at the top end of a down pipe, or at the lower end where it terminates in a bend connected via an underground chain to a soakaway. At the top, debris can be cleared by hand, hoed or speared out. The soak-away end is more difficult to get at. However, there is a simple way which will usually clear a blockage without calling in a drainage contractor. Remove the downpipe section or sections down to the one length joined to the bend. Hose or pour water down this until filled or overflowing. Leaves and twigs and other material will gradually float to the top. If it is solidly packed, disturb with a stick long enough to reach the bottom. Hopefully the water will eventually run away and a good flow from the hose will clear the pipe completely. Replace the other sections, and add a wire or plastic dome in the gutter at the top of and over the outlet so that leaves will not again be taken down.

Faulty fixings will obviously have to be put right or replaced.

Corroded or split rainwater pipes should be replaced, but they can be sealed, and providing this is done neatly and is not unsightly, or it is in a situation where it is not easily seen, the following repair could be looked upon as permanent.

Clean the surface and bind round the pipe a previously cut length of self-adhesive bitumen flashing. Smooth down with a flat trowel or other means, so that complete overall contact is made. This will provide a complete water-tight seal, and may be painted over when maintenance is due.

Chapter Three

Exterior Walls

Walls are constructed with two principal purposes in mind. One is to bear the weight of the roof, the other to provide a weather-proof protective barrier to those living inside.

Cavity walls, tile hanging, cladding and renderings are methods by which the penetration of water or moisture is prevented or at least minimised to the extent that no harm is caused. If any of these methods fail to function, damp can occur.

Movement of the roof/wall can open up cracks in rendering or brickwork, letting rain in.

Air-bricks or damp-proof courses may be missing or faulty, or the earth level may be higher than that of the damp-proof course.

External Defects

Deterioration of the building materials may result in a fault that shows internally as a damp patch; occasionally a defect will also be visible externally – this may be unsightly, but may not cause concern to the occupier. It may be however, an indication of greater problems to come.

Efflorescence Some building materials contain varying amounts of water soluble salts, which, when the material becomes wet leach to the surface and, when they dry out, disfigure the appearance of the outside wall with patches of glistening white crystals.

Temporary efflorescence will disappear of its own accord, but if it continues it is a sign that moisture is an active problem, and the source should be identified and cured.

Efflorescence on new clay brickwork is fairly common and should not cause concern as it will eventually become exhausted. In any case, the efflorescence generally can be brushed from the surface.

If the salt cannot be brushed off the cause of the stain may be due to lime bloom.

Lime Bloom White staining on concrete surfaces, surfaces in proximity to concrete, or on materials containing cement, which will not wash off, may be caused by lime. It appears gradually, and is caused by the lime leaching out of the materials, and which is converted to calcium carbonate – chalk.

The remedy is to very carefully remove the stain with a dilute acid, and then wash the surface thoroughly with water.

Surface Erosion The erosion of brickwork may take place for a number of reasons, and the severity of the condition can vary considerably. The brick face may slowly crumble over a period of time, or large pieces may flake off, leading to rapid recessing of the brick surface.

Frost damage or salt contamination are the two most likely causes; some bricks, particularly if underfired, have low resistance to frost. If they become frozen while saturated with water, then damage is likely to occur.

Moisture also plays a large part in the damage resulting from salt contamination. Water dissolves salts contained within the brick, and on drying carries the salts to or near the surface, where they are deposited as crystals which disrupt the brick face.

The answer to curing this condition, is to provide a means of keeping the wall dry. Several methods are available.

If the wall is of cavity construction and severely affected, then the outer leaf can be removed, and re-built, using a brick of higher frost resistance and low sulphate content. This is obviously a very expensive and drastic course of action, and not for the average home owner.

A physical barrier in the form of tiles, cladding or rendering can be erected.

Renderings should only be applied to a firm background or on to lathing, and should be preferably finished with a pebbledash, Tyrolean or rough-cast surface, not a smooth trowelled finish. This again, can be expensive, and will extensively alter the appearance of the property.

In the majority of cases where damage is not too extensive, a waterproofing treatment may be all that is required, using a colourless silicone water-repellent (see page 30) or a coloured decorative waterproof paint. As these are brush-on treatments, they provide a simple remedy, but as with all decoration, they may have to be periodically repeated.

Interior Surfaces

When damp appears on the interior surface of a wall or ceiling, the cause should be isolated so that the correct cure or preventative treatment can be made.

Some causes have already been dealt with in the chapters on roofs, gutters and rain water pipes. Otherwise the dampness might be caused by rain penetration through the wall, or by moisture rising from ground level.

An isolated damp patch could be caused by a defective service pipe, water or central heating pipe or joint. This can be troublesome, particularly if buried within a wall, under a floor, or in the floor screed. Identification may be difficult but the damp patch will be constantly wet, not varying significantly with weather conditions or the seasons. A small localised repair is often the answer to the problem.

Condensation also affects internal walls, and is a major problem in many buildings. Condensation should not be confused with damp penetration, and is dealt with in Chapter 8.

Penetrating Dampness Penetrating dampness is normally associated with rainfall. The position of the damp patch on the inner wall will help to locate the cause of the trouble.

Solid walls present more damp trouble than those constructed with a cavity, which was introduced to overcome problems of penetrating dampness, as well as to improve insulation. A frequent cause found in solid walls is the development of a crack in the external rendering, mortar or brickwork, of the property. This should be repaired using an appropriate mortar mix.

The building could be relying on some form of external cladding of tiles or weatherboard to provide adequate waterproofing. If any such cladding is defective or missing it should obviously be repaired or replaced.

Broken or blocked gutters or downpipes, or faulty flashings could be allowing water to penetrate the wall; defects of this kind have been dealt with in previous sections.

If an isolated fault cannot be identified, it is possible that the building fabric has become excessively porous due to age. Usually occurring shortly after heavy rain, the damp patches may be extensive, but normally restricted to the wall facing the prevailing wind. Many remedies are available to the homeowner, but all involve introducing some form of waterproof skin to the building. This can be done by some form of cladding,

Weatherboarding

Mortar bridging cavity, which will carry moisture to internal wall

weatherboards, tiling or rendering, or by applying a waterproof decorative material or colourless water repellent.

Penetrating dampness in cavity wall construction usually takes the form of circular stains, which indicate dirty wall ties, rubble, brick or cement bridging the cavity, or the omission or incorrect placement of cavity trays or vertical damp-proof courses allowing moisture to cross from the outer leaf to the inside.

It may be difficult, but if possible, the obstruction should be cleared by removing a few bricks from the outer wall, clearing the offending material, and replacing the bricks. Otherwise a water repellent treatment is the only answer.

In some instances, for reasons of energy saving, the space within the wall may have been filled with insulating material. Such materials are waterproof, and in the majority of instances do not create damp problems. But shrinkage or settlement may well develop fissures, which convey moisture across the cavity.

A colourless water repellent applied to the external wall will generally overcome the problem, but it can only emphasize the need to employ a reputable firm to carry out a cavity fill operation.

Water Repellent Treatment If a wall has become generally porous and needs exterior overall treatment, without discolouring or altering the appearance of the wall, apply a colourless silicone water repellent. This type of product is suitable for use on all vertical porous building surfaces, and will help preserve and provide a water repellent surface, without sealing the surface and trapping moisture in the structure.

Preparation Remove all dirt and loose material. If the surface is washed down, wetting agents or detergents should not be used.

Repair any cracks, defective pointing, guttering, or flashings to make sure water cannot enter because of such faults.

Application Most colourless water repellents on the market are ready to use but with some, dilution is advised and the manufacturer's instructions should be followed.

Best results are obtained when the weather has been dry for three to four days and is likely to remain dry for five to six hours after treatment. Most water repellents will, however, give satisfactory results if applied to damp surfaces, provided the surface is not wringing wet or covered with a film of water.

Apply the repellent liberally over the whole area by means of a soft brush, or low pressure spray with a coarse nozzle, starting at the top and working downwards.

One application is normally sufficient to give a completely effective treatment. Very porous surfaces should be treated with a second coat before the first has dried, approximately four to six hours after the first application.

Paints If it is desired not only to waterproof the wall but provide a decorative colour as well, exterior grade emulsion paints are available, which not only provide some degree of waterproofing, but also give an attractive finish.

Avoid the use of oil-based gloss paints, they provide a total seal which will prevent moisture within the wall from evaporating.

Before applying exterior grade emulsion paints, the receiving surface should be thoroughly prepared: repointing any cracks where necessary, and cleaned to remove dirt and any loose material. The paint should then be applied in one or more coats at the coverage rates advised by the manufacturer or supplier.

If it is felt necessary to use a silicone water repellent in conjunction with an exterior grade emulsion it is important to apply the paint prior to the silicone treatment. If the water repellent is applied first, it may seriously affect the adhesion of the paint.

Colourless silicone water repellent applied to external brickwork

Chapter Four

Interior Walls

Rising Damp

Rising damp is identified by one or more of several symptoms. Moisture from the ground can percolate up a wall to approximately one metre above ground level, staining decoration, lifting wallpaper, softening plaster, or producing mould or fungi in timber and on wall surfaces.

Generally, buildings are constructed with a damp-proof course, to prevent damp rising. Damp-proof courses consist of a layer of slate, bituminous felt or polythene within the wall at about six inches above the ground level. In older properties a damp-proof course may be non-existent, but even in newer buildings they may become damaged or fail.

Damp patches may occur internally through other faults; condensation or defects in the vertical damp-proof courses at the juncture of the wall and window and door frames may be to blame. These faults are dealt with in chapter 5. Ensure correct diagnosis of the problem has been made before planning appropriate remedial work.

Rising dampness can be treated in a number of ways. Before selecting and commencing a cure, one should inspect the situation thoroughly from both sides of the wall. The damp inside may be caused, for example, by the physical bridging of the damp-proof course, and often a cure can be to simply remove the outside offending material.

Soil or sand, piled against an exterior wall, or concrete laid higher than damp-proof courses is often to blame. Remove the material to well below the damp-proof course level.

Cavity walls are not immune from this type of defect, irregular patches of rising dampness, particularly in new buildings, may be a sign that rubble or mortar has collected within the cavity at or above the damp-course level. In this case bricks should be removed, usually from the external leaf of the wall, and the cavity cleared to several inches below the damp proof course.

When building paths, or other construction, adjacent to a wall, it is sometimes found that there is concrete or soil higher than the damp-proof course. Here an external vertical damp barrier can be installed from the existing damp-proof course to 150 mm (6″) above the new intended level. The simplest method to achieve this is to apply two brush coats of bitumen/latex emulsion on to the wall, which should then be protected with a sand/cement render prior to back-filling with soil. Ideally, the vertical membrane should terminate in a horizontal damp-proof course at the higher level to prevent moisture entering the building.

Treatment for Rising Damp Rising damp can be prevented by one of several methods.

These involve inserting a new damp-proof membrane of a physical nature, or by using electro-osmotic or chemical systems.

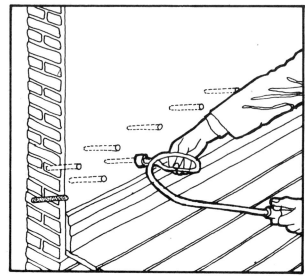

Dampness caused by material piled against external wall – allowing moisture to by-pass damp-proof course

Injecting a chemical damp-proof course

Of the three choices the first is considered to be the most effective but is difficult and time consuming for the average property owner; the chemical injection method being by far the most suitable for do-it-yourself installation.

Increasing sub-soil draining may also be effective in reducing the problem and may be considered in association with one of the above methods of cure.

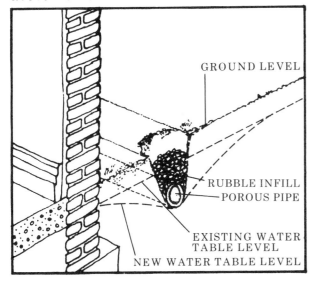

Depressing the water table by increasing sub-soil drainage

Physical Damp-proof Courses

Faulty or non-existent damp-proof courses were at one time replaced or installed by removal of a course of bricks which were replaced after a new damp-proof course had been laid. More recent developments in installation techniques involve cutting a narrow slit with a tungsten tipped chain saw or grinding disc along a mortar joint and inserting a new damp proof course, of copper sheeting, bituminous felt, or polythene. Due to the weight and loading of the wall, obviously only a small section can be carried out at one time, usually from 500 mm to 1 m runs (18″ to 39″); the cut is finally wedged and grouted with mortar.

This system does present some difficulties, it is a disruptive process to carry out and extreme care is required to prevent wall settlement and bricks becoming dislodged. Installation is best left to the professional!

Electro-Osmotic Process This system of preventing rising damp, although far less hazardous than the previous method as it only involves cutting shallow slots, is also invariably carried out by a contractor. It is suitable for most wall constructions, particularly those of considerable thickness.

The passive system involves the planting of continuous soft copper wall electrodes at damp course level, and connecting these to copper coated steel earthing rods driven in the soil.

This produces an electric cell, the low voltages of which prevent moisture from rising through the capillaries within the building material. Applied potential active systems are also available and are developed from the above process; a low voltage is applied in such a way as to increase the effectiveness with which the process depresses rising damp. Although still available, it must be pointed out that the electro-osmotic process has been phased out by at least one well-known contractor, because of its cost effectiveness when compared with other methods of damp proofing.

Chemical Injection Method This method also can be installed by a contractor, or be successfully attempted by a reasonably competent householder.

Basically, a silicone water-repellent is injected under pressure or by gravity, into a series of holes drilled into the wall at specified intervals. The solution spreads outwards left and right from each injection, and thus creates a horizontal damp proof course at the base of the wall.

Application of Chemical Injection Method The chemical injection of a wall can be carried out from either side. It is usual to find that dampness has caused skirting boards to rot, and internal plastered surfaces to deteriorate to such an extent that replacement is essential; treatment from inside is preferred. Where the treatment is necessary the skirtings and lower levels of the internal plasterwork should be removed – preferably a few days before the impregnation treatment is to be applied, to help the wall structure to dry out.

Holes of 16 mm – 20 mm ($\frac{5}{8}''$ to $\frac{3}{4}''$) diameter are drilled into the mortar, or at approx. 230 mm (9") centres in stonework, in two layers immediately above the floor or damp-course level (see page 32). The holes should be drilled to about 20 mm ($\frac{3}{4}''$) from the further side of the wall. Do NOT drill right through.

To ensure holes are drilled each time to the correct and same depth, one can wind insulation tape – or similar – round the drill, leaving exposed the depth required.

When the holes are drilled they should be blocked with corks or rubber bungs having a small hole through the centre, these are available from chemists or home brew shops.

A pressure sprayer (eg. garden type) can be used for injection; the nozzle is removed and the end of the lance is pushed through the hole in the bung, and the water repellent injected, saturating the wall area surrounding the hole. This will become visually obvious when the repellent comes to the surface, for the wall will look as though it is sweating. The time taken to saturate the wall varies considerably, dependent on the porosity of the structure, but not more than 2–5 minutes on average. When one area has been saturated the tube is removed, inserted into the next hole and the process repeated.

As an alternative to the above, impregnation can be carried out more rapidly using a hired electric pressure pump with leads being fed into the holes. Saturation will be reached in a few seconds using this method.

When the required area has been treated, the holes are plugged with a sand/cement mortar. After a minimum of 24 hours, the exposed line of the impregnated wall is then given a brush coat of the water-repellent both internally and externally. When this treatment has been completed, the wall should be left for not less than a week, before internal rendering, plaster, and skirting boards are replaced or decorating is commenced.

If the installation is made by a contractor, a detailed specification for replacing the internal plaster will often be given. This should be accepted and adhered to as otherwise any guarantee given will be invalidated.

The amount of repellent needed can vary greatly depending on the porosity and thickness of the wall. Initially, however, for calculating the quantity needed, three litres per metre run of wall is a fair estimate.

The above treatments are based upon the wall being of solid construction. Should such a treatment be necessary for cavity walls, both internal and external skins should be treated separately. The external one will have to be drilled and impregnated from the outside.

Trench Drainage The effects of rising damp can be reduced, and in minor cases cured completely, by lowering the water table by means of sub-soil drainage. This is achieved by digging a trench around the building, and laying perforated or porous pipes to carry water away into a natural watercourse, or where permitted, to a drain or sewer (see page 33). The depth to which the trench will have to be dug will depend on soil conditions. The placement of the drain should be between 1.5–5 m (5' to 15') away from the affected walls. When excavating, care must be taken to avoid interfering with the stability of the foundations.

Interior Vertical Damp-proof Membranes

When damp conditions exist in internal situations, and for one reason or another it is impossible or impractical to cure the problem at source, a waterproof barrier can be installed by means of an internal skin or membrane.

The choice of treatments available are varied from the simple application of a waterproofing paint to more complicated procedures. The severity of the conditions must, however, be taken into consideration when making a choice.

Bitumen/Latex Emulsions For severe conditions or permanent cure of damp penetration, two procedures are possible by do-it-yourself methods.

The first and possibly the simplest is to apply a bitumen latex membrane. To do this all plaster should first be removed from the areas to be treated, down to the brickwork. The receiving surface must be sound, clean and smooth. For example where mortar courses have crumbled away, a skim coat of cement mortar should be applied to provide a

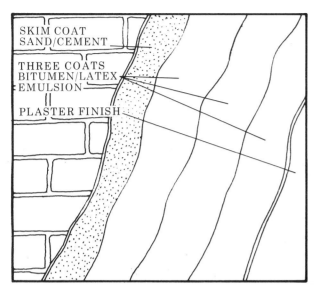

Procedure for applying a vertical damp-proof membrane with a bitumen latex emulsion

Plastering over an internal lath barrier

smooth surface.

The bitumen latex emulsion should be applied to the prepared surface by brush, in two coats, at approximately 1–1.5 sq m per litre per coat, the first being allowed to dry before the second is applied.

The bitumen latex membrane should join with any existing damp-proof course in the walls or membrane in solid floors, so as to form a continuous membrane. Whilst the second coat is still wet it should be blinded with clean, sharp sand to provide a key for the new plaster.

Subsequent plastering should be in two coats, using a lightweight plaster.

Internal Lath Barrier A vertical damp-proof membrane can also be installed by the use of a lath which is fixed directly on to the damp walls. Normally supplied in rolls and manufactured from pitch fibre, the lathing has a dovetail corrugation, which forms a series of air ducts behind the lath when fixed in position.

When using this type of product, all plaster should be removed back to brickwork or masonry and the lath placed against the wall with the corrugations in a vertical position. The lath should be raised slightly away from solid floors or extended beneath a suspended wooden floor to allow complete circulation of air under the lath. Fix in position by nailing with galvanised clout or hardened masonry nails.

The treatment should continue almost to ceiling height where a small gap should be left for air circulation.

Ensure that vertical joints in the treatment are lapped, and that where butt joints are necessary (i.e. horizontal joints) a strip of bitumen felt is fixed behind the joint.

Areas where the lath has to be tailored around pipes or electrical fittings, should be treated with a waterproof mastic, to ensure that no bridging occurs between the new finish and the damp wall.

Once the lath is in position it can be over-plastered, or finished using panel boards, ensuring that the air gaps at the top and bottom of the wall are not obstructed. The gaps can be concealed by skirting boards or coving at ceiling level.

Internal Surface Treatments

For a number of reasons the previously mentioned membranes or barriers may be undesirable; it may be a question of cost, if a surveyor or builder has to be involved, or it may be that the occupants of a property are not the owners and the lowest investment only is desirable. Alternatively the conditions may not be severe enough to warrant dismantling internal wall surfaces.

Surface damp proofing is possible by simple means and various proprietary products are available for application. These will not cure the dampness but will cover the effected areas to resist damp penetrating and spoiling decorations.

Paints (Damp-proof) The most common damp-proofing paints are formulated from chlorinated rubber. They are easy to apply by ordinary paint brush, to any sound, smooth damp or dry surface.

Chlorinated rubber should not be used however where efflorescence salts, which can disrupt the treatment, are evident.

Efflorescence happens in situations where water soluble salts are carried by the dampness to the surface of the affected wall. These salts occur naturally in some building materials, and are generally present in the soil beneath the building. The flow of moisture from the source of dampness to the wall surface, where it evaporates, increases the concentration of the salts at this point, and they form a white crystaline deposit, often disrupting paint films.

Efflorescence should not be confused with the mould or fungi which can at times cover a surface with a white hair-like growth. In situations where efflorescence has been identified, use a laminate paper or foil lining, described later (page 37), or some form of treatment that will provide a mechanically strong barrier.

As with all paint systems, chlorinated rubber products must be applied on to a clean, well-prepared base. Existing wallpaper and paint should be removed, and any mould or fungus on the wall should be destroyed with a suitable fungicide. Defective sections of plaster must be repaired and high spots rubbed down to avoid flaws in the treatment.

Application Apply with an ordinary paint brush to an area appreciably larger than the present dampness, to allow for any subsequent spread. Ensure no drips or runs occur. On damp surfaces brush the first coat well in to obtain good adhesion. One coat may be sufficient, but a second coat is to be recommended, and is essential where appreciable dampness is experienced. Twenty-four hours should be allowed between coats where possible.

These paints can be used on cellar and basement walls provided there is no water

Damp-proofing an internal wall with chlorinated rubber paint

pressure, which will cause the treatment to blister and part company from the wall surface.

Chlorinated rubber paints, contain a solvent which gives off heavy vapours and therefore good ventilation must be maintained during application. To avoid tainting, remove any nearby food until the treatment is dry, when it is odourless.

Once the treated surface is dry, decoration can be applied. Oil-based, and most emulsion paints adhere perfectly. Adhesion of wallpapers will be improved if the treated surface is first painted with an emulsion paint and heavy-duty paste used for paper hanging.

In severe conditions or where efflorescence salts are in evidence, laminate papers and special moisture curing polymer resins can provide an answer.

Moisture Curing Polymers Specially formulated, these products are normally liquids, based on a urethane resin and which can be applied by brush. Absorbed into the substrate, they harden by a chemical process, reacting with moisture or water vapour to form a very hard waterproof barrier.

As with other processes, surface preparation is important; all loose material must be removed, together with any paint or other coating that will prevent absorption of the product. Repairs to mortar or plasterwork should be made to provide a surface suitable to accept the damp-proofing treatment.

Application usually requires three or four coats; very often the first coat will totally disappear into the substrate providing good adhesion for subsequent coats.

Moisture-cured urethanes are suitable for use in problem areas, for example, in basements and cellars, but care should be taken when treating surfaces that are saturated with water, as this could prevent absorption of the resin. In such a situation an artificial method of providing temporarily dry conditions, such as a fan heater, should be employed, to ensure that the surface can absorb sufficient waterproofer to form an adequate bond.

Using wallpapering techniques, damp problems are eliminated with a laminate paper

Laminate Papers and Foils These materials provide an inexpensive means of damp-proofing although they are a little more complex in their application than the other surface treatments mentioned. They will overcome damp problems when associated with efflorescence salts, but may not prove effective in situations involving actual water pressure.

Laminate papers are supplied in rolls and usually with a special adhesive, by which the laminate is stuck to the wall.

Surface preparation must be thorough, existing wallpaper, loose paint or distemper should be removed, and defective plaster repaired to produce a sound, smooth surface. Defects in the surface can not only look unsightly but could pierce the treatment.

The laminate paper can be hung vertically or horizontally, although the former is easier when dealing with large wall sections. The manufacturer's recommendations regarding priming and adhesive application should be strictly adhered to; ensure that adequate overlap (approx. $\frac{1}{2}''$) is provided at joins to prevent damp from penetrating at these areas.

When dry, laminates may be wallpapered over, although very heavy vinyl papers should be avoided.

A difficult problem, successfully treated with a moisture cured polyurethane

Chapter Five

Windows and Doors

Window and Door Frames

Many of the defects associated with windows, doors and their frames are the result of poor construction, maintenance, or lack of inspection. A little time spent in correcting minor faults can prevent many serious problems; whereas if left unattended, small defects can cause deterioration or rot, which will lead to major repairs being necessary, and may allow dampness to penetrate inside the building.

Paint in poor condition will allow water to saturate joinery, and if this is not checked, decay will result. Regular painting of such areas as windows and doors together with fascias and weatherboardings to keep moisture out is essential.

Paint however does not adhere well to damp wood. Paint films that fail early in their life, by cracking, blistering or flaking may indicate that moisture has gained access into the woodwork. Painting damp wood must obviously be avoided, as this only seals in dampness, which will lead to a very early failure of the paint system.

Inspect putty surrounding glass to see if it has shrunk back from the glazing; if so remove it and replace with new material. Check also inside to ensure that moisture that condensates on window panes cannot enter the frame because of a similar fault in the back putty. Check joinery to establish if cracks have opened due to shrinkage or movement, and repair if necessary with a suitable wood filler before painting.

When dealing with damp frames and fittings, wood should always be inspected for rot. Wet rot can cause extensive damage and severely weaken the assembly. All wood affected by rot must be cut away (see chapter 9) and be replaced with new woord or a suitable wood filler. It may often be more economic to totally replace extensively damaged units.

Although the above comments are mainly aimed at wooden construction, metal windows can be effected by corrosion. Prior to the 1940's, metal window frames were not always suitably treated to prevent rust. Corrosion causes paint films to lift and the metal to expand and warp, and which places a strain on glass, causing it to crack for no apparent reason. The only alternative remedy to installing new window frames is to remove all the glass and to eliminate rust with a good rust-inhibitive treatment prior to reglazing and repainting.

Dampness on internal surfaces surrounding window and door joinery may be because of a failure in the damp-proof course and trays surrounding the frames.

Curing faults in the damp-proofing may involve fairly extensive building work, and the services of a competent builder may be required. Fortunately, such problems are not common, and may occur only in new buildings where a damp-proof membrane may have been incorrectly installed or damaged during construction, in which case the house-builder should be eligible.

Heads The head of the frame will be protected by an immediately overhanging roof or by a cavity tray (see 'abutments' page 24). The cavity tray should collect any moisture that has penetrated the outer leaf of the wall, but if it is defective, the moisture will enter the building and show as a damp patch above the window or door frame. Fortunately, the increasing use of metal lintels with an integral tray, has almost eliminated this type of failure.

Damp symptoms can however, be seen if mortar – even small pieces – have become lodged on the tray in such a way as to bridge the cavity, allowing moisture from the wet outer leaf to penetrate to the inner skin. The effect produced is similar to that caused by dirty wall ties (see page 30), and can be overcome by clearing the cavity in the same way.

Jambs Where a window or a door is inserted in a cavity wall, it is necessary to provide a closure in the cavity, and the outer and the inner wall will come into contact. Moisture is prevented from gaining access to the interior wall by means of a vertical damp-proof course, which is fixed to the frame and runs between the cavity closure and the external wall, and extends into the cavity.

When windows are installed during wall construction, effective damp-proofing by the above method is relatively easy to achieve; but a failure can occur if replacement windows are fitted, or the windows are installed, after the completion of the wall. Care is

Metal lintel with combined cavity tray

Jamb, with damp-proof course inserted in cavity closure

needed to ensure that the damp-proof material is not damaged, and is correctly tucked into a rebate at the side of the frame (see above).

Incorrect installation or damage to the damp-proof material in the jambs will often lead to dampness in the reveal adjacent to the frame. Remedial work to correct or re-place the materials will provide the only permanent cure.

If the reveal exhibits minor dampness only, particularly after wind-driven rain, it may be wise to inspect the outside of the frame where it butts against the exterior wall. The gap between the wall and the frame may be filled with a fillet of sand and cement or mastic, as the original mortar may have become cracked or may have fallen away completely.

A gap round a window or door frame is not normally critical, as the damp-proof course in the jambs should provide protection against the weather; it may even be advisable to allow a free flow of air to the back of the frame where the joinery can come into contact with the damp brickwork.

In cases where the damp-proof course is not firmly fixed to, or tucked well into, a rebate in the frame, the application of a sealant to fill the gap between frame and wall, may stop the penetration of wind-blown rain into the structure. This is a simple operation, and will be considerably cheaper than attempting to correct any fault within the damp-proof course.

There are many proprietary brands available from builders' merchants and DIY shops. Choose one that claims to be flexible after drying, and will not harden only to fall out again. These sealants are often supplied in cartridges for gun application, and some dealers loan guns for a small deposit. The sealants are available in a range of colours, but most can be overpainted within a few hours of application.

Once faults to window and door frames are corrected, it must be remembered that the original damp patch will not immediately disappear. The wall may remain damp for some time, and to prevent any new decoration being damaged or stained, coat over the damp area with a chlorinated rubber paint (see page 36).

Doors, if not protected by a porch, should be fitted with a weatherboard at the bottom to throw off rain; this also should incorporate a drip groove, otherwise water may trickle inside or cause decay to the step below.

A weatherboard is an obvious attachment to make, and is not usually omitted. The board should be fitted so that rain does not run behind it, and if possible extended sufficiently to throw the rain beyond the door step. Ready-made weatherboards are available in DIY shops or timber merchants, and are easily cut to the width of the door.

Window Sills A damp patch internally, below the window, may point to yet another fault, which can be easily rectified. Once again inspect the window from outside. The window sill arrangement is designed to carry rain away from the building. Examine the underside of any timber sill, where a drip groove running its entire length should be found. The groove is to prevent water from tracking back along the underside and saturating brickwork; but it will obviously not function if it has been filled with mortar, dirt, or repeated applications of paint. Cleaning out the groove should be an easy operation. If no groove can be found then cutting one may be difficult, but should be within the capability of most.

Sills on older property may be formed from concrete or tiles; any cracks in the concrete which let in water should be filled with an appropriate waterproof filler. Cracked or broken tiles should be replaced and all joints made watertight.

The sill itself should sit on a damp-proof membrane; this should isolate the sill from the wall beneath, and prevent any water which may penetrate the assembly from reaching the inside of the building. The sill will have to be removed in order to examine or correct a fault with the damp-proof membrane; with this problem, it would be advisable to consult a builder.

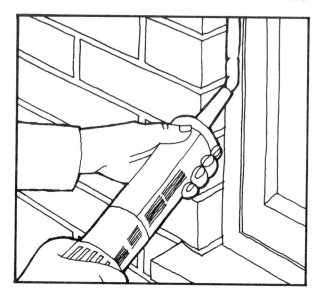

Flexible sealants can be applied from a cartridge to seal area between frame and brickwork

Chapter Six

Floors

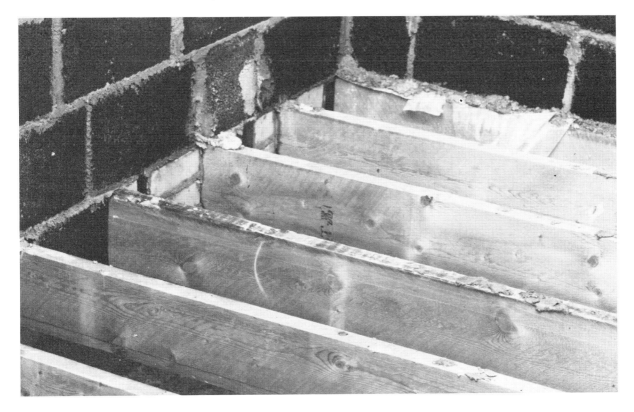

Floors at ground level in domestic buildings are either of timber or are of solid construction. Floors to upper storeys are normally constructed of boarding or chipboard on wooden joists, although in some instances, mainly in high rise buildings, pre-cast concrete units are used.

When damp problems exist, first determine, particularly with solid floors, that condensation is not the cause of dampness – see pages 47–50.

Problems in upper storeys When floors in upper storeys exhibit dampness it is usually a symptom of a fault in some other part of the building fabric. Check for leaking water-pipes, wash basin or W.C. Inspect external walls to ensure that rain penetration is not occurring due to cracks, faulty pointing or leaky gutters and downpipes – see relevant sections for remedial measures.

Timber Floors

Ground Floors Timber floors are supported by joists which rest on sleeper walls or are sometimes let into external walls. The joists should be protected from dampness by a damp-proof course of lead, zinc, slate or bitumen impregnated felt. The space beneath the floor is not an accident of design but provides essential ventilation, the air passing through air bricks in the external walls to keep the moisture content of the wood low and so prevent fungal attack.

Damp Symptoms Damp in timber floors is frequently accompanied by fungal or insect attack. These conditions are discussed in the chapter dealing with timber protection – see pages 51–55.

Dealing with damp only, the areas which are affected can provide an indication as to the cause of the problem. If the dampness is general, then inadequate ventilation must be suspected. In this case, damp, stagnant air beneath the floor encourages mould and fungus to develop on the underside of the floor and often the first indication of trouble is a dank musty aroma.

If the dampness is localised and adjoining a wall (though it must be accepted that the wall below the damp-proof course will remain wet) then rising dampness or water penetration from outside is indicated. Check to ensure the problem is not caused by a leak in a pipe or fitting.

In many cases the first signs of trouble may be seen under floor coverings, the boards under linoleum or carpet may show signs of dampness, yet surrounding areas may appear dry; this is simply because the floor coverings retain the moisture, whereas elsewhere the moisture evaporates and dries out.

Remedies: Underfloor Check air bricks from outside the house. They should be placed immediately below the damp-proof course, and so positioned that every below ground area is ventilated. Ensure they are functioning and not blocked by earth or rubble or have been deliberately blocked to prevent draughts or mice entering. There should be one airbrick for every six feet in external walls, ensuring a constant cross-flow of fresh air; if there is not this number, ventilation is likely to be inadequate and the additional airbricks should be installed.

Further investigation will require a few floor boards to be removed. Choose those that are the most damp or in the worst condition. Examine the under floor space to ensure that rubble or soil is not piled up sufficiently to conduct moisture to the joists or boards themselves, or are interrupting the free flow of air under the floor. The areas adjacent to walls should also be inspected to ensure that any rubble is not bridging the damp-proof course and so causing trouble.

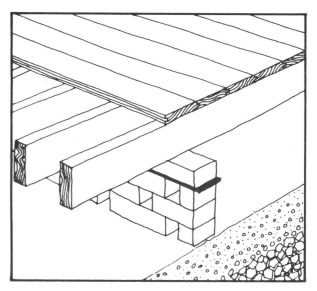

Supports for floor joists (if any) should incorporate a damp-proof membrane

This is also a good time to look at the underside of the floorboards to evaluate the extent of any damage which may have been caused by rot. For treatment see the section on protection of timber.

Examine the joists at their supports; particularly inspect the damp-proof course material which should be placed below the joists or, if there is one, under the timber plate.

Joists supported on sleeper walls should also be isolated by means of a damp-proof material; an effective damp-proof course can be introduced using bitumen impregnated felt or lengths of self-adhesive flashing.

Once the source of moisture has been established and resolved, all remaining or replacement timber, joists, floorboards or skirting boards together with areas of adjacent brickwork exposed to rot or fungus should be liberally treated with a good preservative – see chapter 9.

Solid Floors

Solid floors are built from concrete with a sand/cement topping screed, and damp-proofing is usually effected by means of a damp-proof membrane, usually of polythene or a bituminous material underneath or sandwiched in its construction.

Building regulations normally only require

Ensure air bricks allow ventilation to underfloor areas, unblock if necessary

the provision of a damp-proof membrane in solid floors, if the floor finish is to be of timber or similar susceptible material, as these would be affected by moisture vapour. Even where a damp-proof membrane has been provided, it may have been damaged during construction or badly fitted.

Symptoms Vapour penetration of solid floors can be identified by a change in appearance of the floor covering. Indeed if the concrete is left exposed, as in garage floors for example, the dampness may not be identified in its early stages as the surface readily dries by evaporation.

Damage caused to wood block flooring by an ineffective damp-proof membrane

If a damp-proof membrane has not been fitted, wood block flooring will absorb the moisture and expand, causing the blocks to tilt in places.

Thermoplastic or vinyl asbestos tiles may also become loose, usually because the moisture becomes alkaline as it passes upward through the concrete, and this can attack and break down the adhesive used to fix the tiles.

Clay tiles may also distort and lift. Sheet floor coverings, if fully bonded to the concrete floor may ripple or blister.

Open weave, loose-laid coverings should not be affected, but the underside of an impervious sheet covering such as vinyl or linoleum will become damp.

Rising dampness can also be induced by water being absorbed by the floor screed in other ways. Excessive quantities of water used when cleaning floors should be avoided, and checks should be made to ensure that faulty plumbing or other possible causes are not to blame, before a course of remedial action is decided upon.

Remedies Treatment may often involve removing the floor or providing a topping screed and, in either case incorporating an effective damp-proof membrane, for which, a number of alternative materials are available. The most widely used being polythene, hot bitumen, bitumen/latex emulsions, mastic asphalt or bitumen sheeting.

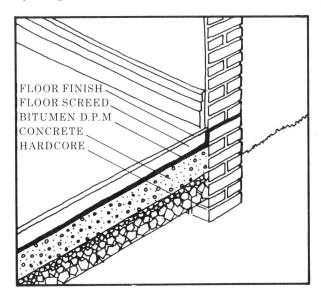

FLOOR FINISH
FLOOR SCREED
BITUMEN D.P.M
CONCRETE
HARDCORE

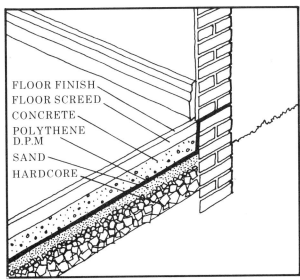

FLOOR FINISH
FLOOR SCREED
CONCRETE
POLYTHENE D.P.M
SAND
HARDCORE

Position of damp-proof membranes in conventional solid floor construction

43

Mastic asphalt is probably the most effective of the damp-proofing materials, but it is difficult for the layman to install as special skill and heating equipment is required, and is not used to any great extent in domestic situations.

Similarly with bitumen sheet materials, although their performance is beyond question, installation can prove to be difficult.

The equipment necessary to provide a membrane with hot-applied bitumen may also restrict its use by the house owner.

The remaining two methods, polythene and bitumen/latex emulsions can be easily applied. They are both readily available from builders' merchants and fairly simple to install.

Bitumen/latex probably provides the most effective vapour barrier and for this reason, instructions on its application are given. The method for using polythene is similar, the polythene sheeting is loose laid on a bed of sand prior to laying the concrete slab. This is to minimise as much as possible the risk of puncturing the membrane during the laying.

Incorporating a Bitumen/Latex Membrane in New Solid Floors The existing floor must be dug out to provide sufficient room for the replacement one to be installed. Generally this entails removal of the existing floor to a level up to 12″ below the required final floor level.

Sufficient hardcore should then be laid to raise the level to that required, and compacted. On this the main slab of concrete 4″ deep should be laid, levelled and allowed to harden.

The surface should then be coated with a bitumen/latex emulsion, applied by brush at the rate of approximately 1 sq. metre per litre and allowed to dry. Care must be taken to ensure the coating is taken up walls to marry with any existing damp-proof course in the surrounding walls.

A second application should then be applied at 1½ sq. metres per litre and as this dries it can be blinded with clean sharp sand as a protection against damage, and to provide a key for the top screed. If damage does occur to the membrane at this stage it can easily be repaired by further coats of emulsion.

When the bitumen/latex emulsion has fully dried a top finishing sand/cement screed at least 50 mm (2″) should be laid over the membrane.

Once the final screed has dried the required floor finish can be added to complete the job.

Surface Sealants It may not be expedient to disturb an existing floor to install a new damp-proof membrane, as the work involved may be too much in either cost or labour.

Surface sealing is a possibility but the required performance is demanding. The product used must be capable of providing a vapour barrier, be strong enough to resist physical damage, and have a good bond strength to damp concrete.

One product that meets these requirements is moisture-cured polyurethane. It penetrates deeply, bonds perfectly with concrete, and has the additional benefit of preventing surface dusting – a common problem, particularly with garage floors.

Application The floor must be thoroughly clean and free from any material that will prevent absorption of the polyurethane into the concrete. Any surface irregularities can be made good by priming the areas concerned with the moisture-cured polyurethane, and then filling with a mortar, prepared by mixing 6-parts dry sand, 1-part cement and 1-part polyurethane (measured by volume). Only sufficient material should be mixed that can be used within twenty minutes, as after that period the mix stiffens and is difficult to handle.

When a sound surface has been achieved, apply the moisture-cured polyurethane over the entire floor by brush, at the rate of 1.8 kg per 10 square metres. Three coats are normally required, each being applied at intervals of two to three hours, when the previous coat is tack free, but not fully cured.

Once the final coat is applied complete chemical hardening takes place, and after six to eight hours the polyurethane is sufficiently hard enough to provide a walkable

Surface waterproofing a solid concrete floor with a
moisture cured urethane

surface. Complete hardening takes place
within forty-eight hours, to provide a tough,
resilient surface, with good resistance to
wear and to many chemicals, as well as oil and
grease.

Chapter Seven

Basements

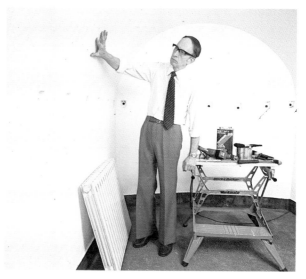

Whether a basement is wholly or partly below ground level, the problems incurred with dampness require special attention. Basements are normally associated with older properties and the damp-proofing techniques employed during construction were often inadequate, with poor ventilation resulting in a damp uninhabitable atmosphere. It is probable that every surface except the ceiling will require attention.

Dampness is invariably due to the walls and floor taking in moisture from the surrounding ground. Treatment is often virtually impossible from the external side of the building, and effective damp-proofing must be installed to totally seal the internal surfaces. One this is accomplished, ventilation, background heating and, if possible, insulation should be provided to prevent condensation from occurring on the walls and floors (see chapter 8).

Basement floors vary in their construction; brick and flagstones are common, and treatment may necessitate their removal and a new concrete floor laid (chapter 6). If the floor is of concrete and in reasonable condition it may be used as the sub-floor, providing no inconvenience is caused by the extra inches in height required, or be treated with a moisture cured polymer (page 36).

It should never be assumed that there is no dampness associated with a basement floor. If the floor has been left exposed and appears satisfactory it may only be because surface dampness is drying out by evaporation. A simple test can be made by covering an area of the floor with an impervious sheet such as plastic or metal foil, sealing the edges. Remove this after twenty-four hours, and inspect the floor and the back of the sheet for signs of dampness.

Basement Walls If the walls show only moderate signs of dampness, and are not subjected to actual water pressure they can be sealed in a number of ways with a surface treatment as outlined on page 36.

Those in a more serious condition will require a vertical damp-proof membrane (page 35) to be installed. Where possible such membranes should be extended to join with the membrane in the floor and continue upward to marry with any existing damp-proof course in the brickwork above ground level.

Dampness in basement walls cannot be cured by chemical injection or any other form of damp-proof course installed at the lower levels of the walls, as dampness is, of course, penetrating at all levels.

Chapter Eight

Condensation

Condensation is a major problem in many homes. It is brought about by a number of causes and its control is far from simple.

Houses appear to suffer from condensation more today than in the past, and this is not an illusion. It is an unfortunate fact due to changes in our living habits, and the use of modern building materials and design techniques.

An understanding of why condensation occurs is necessary to identify the problem and to ensure that a correct diagnosis is made.

Water vapour is produced in our homes by many processes; cooking, washing, bathing; even a person breathing gives off moisture, adding about one pint of water to the atmosphere every eight hours. We hasten to add however, that it is not proposed the reader foregoes this habit!

Flueless gas and oil heaters and cookers are greater culprits, for though they provide heat, they also produce large quantities of water vapour as they burn.

In our energy-conscious society we now restrict the amount of ventilation in buildings. Double glazing, better fitting windows and doors and more effective draught proofing conserve heat, but reduce ventilation. Central heating is a standard fitting in modern houses and is installed in many older properties; open fires are replaced, as a result of which we no longer obtain the ventilation produced by the chimney. Similarly, solid floors are now commonplace, with a marked reduction in the number of suspended floors, which provided under floor ventilation.

Changes have not only arisen due to design. Living conditions have also altered drastically; many homes are left unoccupied during much of the day, unventilated and unheated. Activities such as washing and cooking, which produce moisture vapour, are crammed into shorter time intervals. High concentrations of water vapour occur during these short periods, and, due to inadequate ventilation, are not dispersed. Cold walls and floors which do not have time to warm up, because of intermittent heating, attract moisture from the atmosphere and the surfaces become saturated.

Relative Humidity The quantity of moisture contained in the air at a particular temperature, is known as the Relative Humidity (r.h.). This is expressed as a ratio between the amount of moisture actually contained in the air and the maximum amount of moisture the air can hold assuming the temperature remains constant.

The maximum amount of moisture that air is capable of holding will alter with temperature, the warmer the air the more moisture it can retain.

The relative humidity of air, therefore, varies not only with the amount of moisture but also with temperature.

Air containing 10 grams of water/kg of air will have a relative humidity of 100% at a temperature of 14°C, i.e. it will be totally saturated. If we increase the temperature, say to 18°C, the relative humidity will drop to 77% which means to reach a total saturation at this new temperature a further 3 grams of water per kilogram of air must be added.

But if the process is reversed and air containing 13 grams of water per kilogram at 18°C (r.h. 100%) is reduced to a temperature of 14°C, the air will contain 3 grams more moisture than it can possibly physically hold.

It is this excess which is shed and deposited and which we know as condensation.

The stage at which air starts to shed excess moisture is known as its dew point.

Symptoms When warm air cools, it will shed the excess moisture which it can no longer hold, and which usually happens when it comes into contact with a cold surface, such as a window or wall. On an impervious surface this can be seen as tiny droplets of water, but when condensation occurs on an absorbent material, it may not be so immediately noticeable. These damp surfaces encourage mould growth and this is frequently associated with condensation.

The damp may not be a permanent feature. It is likely to appear and disappear as the humidity and temperature vary, but the mould remains ready to re-activate and continue to spread when moist conditions return.

Condensation can occur anywhere, the most frequent areas affected are where high levels of water vapour are produced, such as in kitchens and bathrooms. Moisture can however permeate throughout the house to cause damp conditions far from the source of moisture. Condensation can cause clothing, soft furnishings and bedding to become damp and grow mildew.

Rooms which are remote and unheated – bedrooms for example – exhibit the worst conditions. Because of the lack of heating in these rooms, windows are kept closed, and this lack of ventilation aggravates the situation.

It is uncommon to find surface condensation in living areas, as they are invariably heated for several hours during the day, although if air does not circulate thoroughly throughout the room, isolated corners, particularly on outside walls, can suffer.

Condensation may also be produced by sudden changes in weather conditions. For example if warm humid weather follows a cold spell, walls in all parts of the house may run with water. These conditions are generally temporary, and are so infrequent as not to cause any serious problems, and remedial action is rarely needed.

Remedy Architects, builders and designers are now very much aware of conditions that cause condensation, and are doing much to overcome the problem.

This is little consolation to those with homes that are now prone to condensation, and although there are no magic cures for the complaint, there are measures that can be taken, singly or combined that should show at least an improvement.

Mould Mould growths can be removed by washing with a fungicide or a household bleach solution, but unless the conditions which produce the condensation are improved, the mould will soon reappear.

Water Vapour at Source As condensation is caused by excessive water vapour, it is sensible to remove it at its point of origin.

Extractor fans fitted in kitchens and bathrooms can disperse large amounts of water vapour to outside the house, and are relatively inexpensive to run.

Keep bathrooms and kitchen doors closed and tight fitting when these rooms are in use. This will reduce water vapour migrating to other areas.

Heating A low level of continuous background heating helps to combat condensation, much more efficiently than short spells of high temperature. The latter may warm the air quickly but does little to warm the fabric of the building. As has been mentioned, warm air meeting cold walls is an ideal condensation promoting condition.

Heating methods which aggravate and encourage conditions leading to condensation should be avoided. For example, flueless gas appliances and paraffin heaters provide heat, but as they burn produce large volumes of water vapour, and as the cause of condensation, should be shunned if possible.

Insulation Insulation on its own will not reduce condensation but will help to maintain background heating. Ideally, insulation should be placed so as to keep the bulk of the structure warm.

Thin surface insulants, such as expanded sheet polystyrene, do not effectively improve the thermal capacity of the wall, but they are useful when quick, intermittant heating is in use.

It is important to note that plastics are inflammable, and could be the means of rapid fire spread. So if insulating with polystyrene, be sure to use a self-extinguishing grade.

On solid concrete floors – a very cold surface – wood blocks or cork tile flooring provide useful insulation, particularly if laid in a bitumen adhesive.

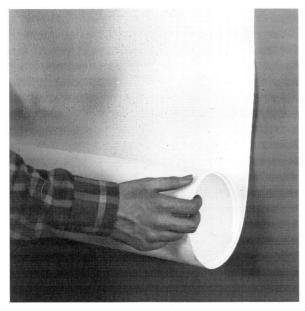

Expanded polystyrene, in sheet form, applied to wall surface, to improve insulation

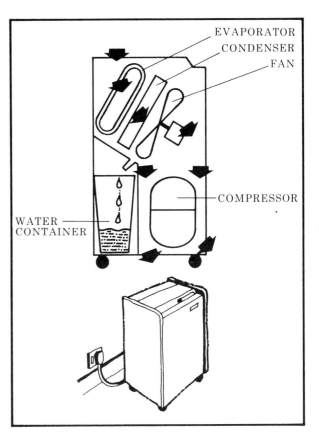

EVAPORATOR
CONDENSER
FAN
COMPRESSOR
WATER CONTAINER

Principle of a dehumidifier in operation

Dehumidifiers

Dehumidifiers remove surplus moisture from the air without, it is claimed, overdrying the atmosphere. A fan draws the damp, moist air from the room and passes it over a cold refrigerated coil, cooling the air so that the moisture condenses and drops into a container inside the cabinet. The dried air then passes over a hot condenser coil and back into the room to re-circulate . . . an additional benefit, helping to keep heating costs down.

Most models automatically switch off to prevent overflowing and a warning light indicates that the water container is full.

Domestic models are reasonably attractively designed in cabinets to fit in a room as furniture pieces. They are portable to plug in any room, and consume on average the electricity needed for two lamp bulbs. When using a dehumidifier, it is not necessary to keep doors or windows open for ventilation.

Ventilation Because of high heating costs, there is often a reluctance to ventilate a room. But effective ventilation can result in a

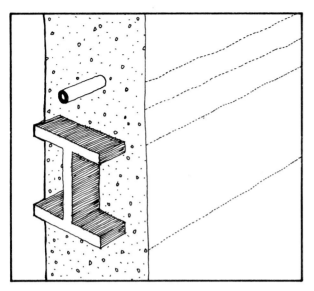

Cold bridging, and the surface condensation which may result due to steelwork or cold water pipes buried within the wall

where a solid concrete or steel member is buried in the width of a wall.

The effect is generally localised, and treated as for normal surface condensation. But for a repair to be effected, correct diagnosis and appropriate action are necessary to reduce the heat loss.

Interstitial Condensation Under certain conditions, condensation will occur unseen inside parts of a building structure, and the effects are not readily noticeable until they become saturated.

In some circumstances, this type of condensation is unwittingly induced by the application of an external vapour seal, paint or other coatings, which prevent a structure from breathing. This then, is to be avoided. Any barrier applied to the exterior should act as a moisture barrier only, and permit vapour trapped in the structure to escape.

The remedy is to provide an *internal* vapour barrier, but if suspected, advice should be sought from a good builder or surveyor.

notable reduction in the level of condensation, with minimal increased heating costs.

Natural ventilation is introduced simply by opening a top window, but better still, by fitting extractor fans.

Air bricks, properly sited, are also effective. They should be placed to provide a through flow of air in the room to prevent stagnant pockets of air accumulating.

Built-in cupboards and wardrobes and airing cupboards prone to condensation should be provided with ventilation at both high and low levels to ensure free air movement.

If full width shelves are incorporated in the design, provide an air gap or perforate at the rear of the shelves, otherwise they will interfere with, and possibly stop the desired airflow.

Defects in Design Two other factors which can lead to condensation must be considered. Their diagnosis can be difficult and the remedy may require skill beyond that of all but the most capable handyman.

These two factors are 'cold bridging' and 'interstitial condensation'. Both are defects in design or construction and usually involve structural alteration to cure, and a reliable builder should be consulted.

Cold Bridging Cold bridging takes place in an isolated area, where the insulation of the structure in that particular spot is less effective than the surrounding areas, for example

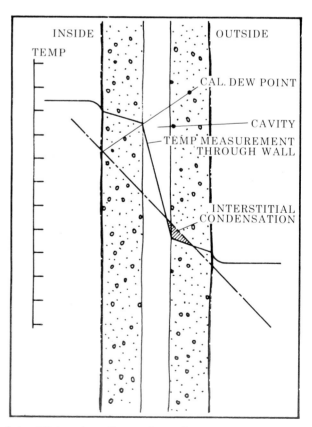

Interstitial condensation can form when temperature falls below dew point

Chapter Nine

Fungi and Insect Attack of Timber

Fungi and insect attack in timber probably causes more anxiety than any other problem. Maybe it is because fungus looks so horrible or one visualises the house crumbling to rubble because of woodworm.

So let's have a calm look at what can happen – and how to cope with the problems that follow.

Fungus Attack

Fungi require certain well-defined conditions for growth and are influenced by temperature, moisture and an adequate supply of food and oxygen.

In common with other plants fungi growth is very dependent on temperature. Ideal conditions are produced between 20–27°C, which means our summer weather is perfect for rapid growth. Lower temperatures restrict development, and growth practically stops around freezing point. Unfortunately fungi are not killed by low temperatures; they become dormant, and re-activate when more favourable warm conditions return. At temperatures in excess of 27°C the growth rate slows, and most common forms of fungi are completely destroyed by temperatures around 65°C.

The moisture content of the average piece of seasoned, air dried wood is approximately 18% by weight, and at this level fungal attack is extremely unlikely. Although rapid growth of decay fungi requires a moisture content in excess of 28%, decay can occur in some wood with a moisture content as low as 24%.

Oxygen is necessary to enable the fungi to break down the complex organic materials on which it feeds. Air pockets within the wood itself can provide sufficient oxygen to meet the requirements of the fungi. It is an interesting fact that water-logged wood does not decay, for this is the only practical method of driving out all the air within the wood, the voids being totally filled with water.

Timber decay in buildings can be caused by a number of different strains of fungi. The most common forms fall into two categories – Wet and Dry rot. It is important to try to distinguish between these two types of decay as the remedial measures differ.

Dry Rot

The term dry rot is somewhat misleading and in the past has been used incorrectly to describe many forms of fungicidal decay. True dry rot is caused by fungi known to science as *Merulius Lacrymans*, which in common with other fungi requires moist conditions in which to thrive. The dry rot fungus does however favour less wet wood than other forms of fungi.

Fairly stable conditions are necessary for the dry rot fungus to develop; fluctuations in temperature or moisture hamper its growth. It is therefore rarely seen outdoors and is unlikely to effect exposed wood, such as roofing timbers, but will thrive in situations such as cellars and on floor timbers.

Once established the dry rot fungi can

The effect of dry rot

cause considerable damage, as it has the ability to spread rapidly, the mycelium (hair-like root system of the fungi) being able to penetrate plaster or brickwork at an alarming rate, spreading from room to room or even from one building to another in its search for new food. The mycelium also have the ability to carry moisture with them, so having gained a hold under moist conditions the fungus can colonise wood which would otherwise be too dry to support active growth. It is understandable why this species causes such concern and why accurate identification and correct remedial measures should be made as early as possible.

Identification When the dry rot fungus attacks timber under damp conditions the wood becomes covered with delicate, white, cotton-like strands, which branch and interweave to form a silky white sheet. Under dryer conditions the colour may vary from white to a light grey and patches of lilac or lemon may develop.

As the colony develops the strands knit together and veins up to 5 mm ($\frac{1}{4}''$) in diameter can often be seen. Fruiting bodies with an irregular pancake shape may develop, varying in colour from yellow to red-brown with generally a white edge. These fruiting bodies are capable of producing many thousands of spores, which can cover adjacent areas with a fine red-brown dust.

As decay continues, the wood darkens in colour and characteristic deep splits occur, both along and across the wood grain, splitting the wood into cubical or brick-shaped pieces. The decayed wood eventually loses weight and strength and crumbles.

In some instances decay may be difficult to diagnose, particularly if the wood has at some time been painted. Here one should look for a general shrinking of the wood, which often causes the paint surface to become dished or wavy. Check the firmness of the wood by using a screwdriver or similar tool; if the wood appears soft and crumbly then decay is indicated.

Cure (Dry Rot) Before considering any treatment, we suggest that if extensive dry-rot is diagnosed, eradication is best left to a professional firm or at least, advice obtained from a surveyor or other expert. As previously mentioned, once established, dry rot spreads mercilessly in all directions and the whole possible area of attack should be investigated. Partial treatment is not satisfactory as further growth will rapidly develop.

This advice applies particularly to older properties, where there may be large areas of panelling and other timber with affected areas out of sight; this has to be found and eradicated. However, if the householder wishes to take matters into his own hands, there are a few basic rules.

Rot is caused initially by the timber becoming damp. Before treating the decay the cause of the dampness must be identified. Examine every aspect of the construction, as detailed elsewhere in this book, to identify all possible points of entry of water, and include in any remedial action an effective cure for the damp problem.

Examine all timbers in the affected area, pay particular attention to joists and rafters, including any sections inserted into the wall or masonry. Probe the timber for soundness. Check wood in adjacent rooms, remember the dry rot fungus in its search for food can penetrate through walls or ceilings and between plaster and brick.

Having determined the extent of the outbreak, all infected timber must be removed; cut away damaged wood plus 300–450 mm (12″–18″) of apparently good wood beyond the area identified. Any remaining wood should be liberally treated with preservative before any replacement timber is inserted.

When dealing with dry rot, walls and masonry in the adjacent area must be sterilised. Several methods are available to the contractor, but the most practical solution is to irrigate the wall with a suitable wood preservative.

First the walls should be thoroughly cleaned and ideally the preserving fluid should be injected under pressure into holes drilled into the wall, until total saturation is achieved. This however, takes large volumes of preserving fluid and total saturation may be very difficult. Two or three applications, by brush or spray, of preservative to the surface of the wall may in many cases be sufficient to check the movement of the fungus, particularly if the initial source of dampness has been eliminated.

As a further precautionary measure, soil or rubble should be removed from beneath effected flooring timbers to a depth of 100–150 mm (4″–6″) and the area sprayed with preservative to endeavour to kill any residual spores and prevent their re-activation.

To complete the work all replacement timbers should also be treated with preservative, and care should be taken to ensure that all debris and material removed from an infestation is cleared from the building, and where possible, destroyed.

The preservative fluid should be easily obtained from most builders' merchants. All proprietary brands of timber treating fluids indicate on the container their purposes, and there will be no problem in choosing one to cope with dry rot. General application details are given under the section detailing wet rot.

In severe cases of rot the strength of constructional timbers must be suspect, and in any cases where timber is cut away, caution must be exercised. Ensure that the building's structure is not weakened in any way, and where necessary, adequate props are provided when undertaking major repairs.

Wet Rot

Wet rot is a general term which covers decay caused by several types of fungi. They attack wood which has become damp and, unlike dry rot, require a relatively high moisture content to grow successfully.

Wet rot fungus

Wet rot is less of a problem to deal with than dry rot. It does not spread over non-timber surfaces and is therefore more easily controlled. If conditions can be induced to stop the moisture at source all further fungus activity ceases without any other cure or treatment, although of course preventative applications of timber preservative is always advisable.

The occurrence of wet rot is usually limited to timber that has become and remained wet for some time. It is therefore not isolated to internal situations, but can effect timbers used externally, particularly those buried in or in close contact with damp soil. Internally, areas prone to attack are joist ends and skirting boards in contact with wet masonry and brickwork, or window and door joinery. **Identification of Wet Rot Attack** As there are a number of different species grouped under this general term, identification can be sometimes confused. In practice only two or three species commonly occur, but more than one species may be present. Fruiting bodies, rarely seen, are sheet-like and normally yellow to olive brown.

Infected wood shrinks and darkens; cracking occurs predominantly along the grain, a thin skin of unaffected wood may cover the decay as the surface may be too dry for attack. The mycellium are thread-like and at first a yellow/white colour, but they soon darken becoming dark brown or even black.

Paint films may mask the condition and if decay is suspected the strength of the timber can be tested with a sharp instrument.

Cure Again, as for dry rot, the first essential is to remedy the defect which has caused the timber to become wet. When this has been done, and if the extent of the rot is minimal, gradual drying will rid the timber of wet rot.

If decay is such that timbers have become unsafe or if diagnosis is uncertain, the timber effected must be cut away. It is advisable, though not essential, to cut away a portion of the adjacent sound timber.

All remaining wood and any replacement timbers should then be treated with a preservation solution.

Application of Preservative Proprietary preservatives carry instructions for use, which should be strictly adhered to, but in general the application for the treatment of wet and dry rot and insect attack is relatively simple.

The timber to be treated should be free from bark, paint, polish or grease and should where possible be treated before placed in its ultimate position.

Once areas affected by fungus have been removed the fluid should be applied by brush or spray to all surfaces, paying particular attention to end grain and fabricated joints. Two coats should be used to ensure maximum penetration of the fluid, the second and any subsequent coats being applied before the previous application has fully dried.

Alternatively timber, if of a convenient size, can be dipped into the preservative, for 3–5 minutes, but ensure that the wood is totally submerged. Any sections of timber that are to be buried or in contact with the ground should be dipped for at least one hour so that total saturation is achieved.

If the treated wood is to be painted or varnished ensure that the correct grade of preservative is used, some cannot be overcoated, and ensure that it is fully dry before painting is attempted.

It is advisable to wear plastic gloves when using wood preservatives; eyes should also be protected. Always ensure adequate ventilation during use. Splashes on the skin can be removed with a hand cleaner and then thoroughly washed with soap and water. Contaminated clothing should be removed immediately and washed before re-wearing. Wood preservatives are toxic materials, and unprotected people and animals must be kept away from treated areas for forty-eight hours or until the treatment is fully dry.

Woodworm (Insect attack of Timber)

Although not strictly a problem caused by dampness, it is an unfortunate fact that very often wood affected by dampness and fungi is also prone to insect attack.

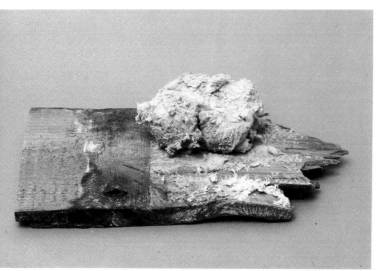

Wet rot fungus growing on wood

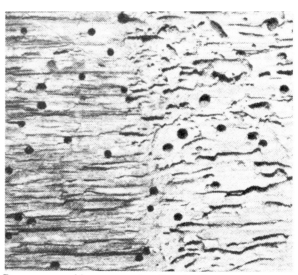

Damage caused by common furniture beetle

Of the many insects which will devour seasoned wood by far the most abundant (and therefore the only one which we will detail) is the common furniture beetle, which will attack the sapwood of most softwoods and hardwoods. It has been shown that they do favour wood with high moisture content, and are rather partial to wood containing some form of fungal decay.

It is therefore not surprising that the two infections are often seen together. If signs of insect attack are found when searching for wet or dry rot, it would obviously be unwise to ignore the fact.

Identification We have all seen the holes left by the furniture beetle when discovered; this does not mean that there is now a colony of beetles munching its way at the fabric of the home; it is a sign that it has been there for the last three to four years. The common woodworm has a complicated life cycle, starting as an egg laid on the surface of the wood. After an incubation period of four to five weeks larva hatches and burrows into the wood, where it feeds producing dust filled tunnels. After several years the larva returns to just under the surface of the wood where it pupates, and after a further six to eight weeks development, an adult emerges from the flight holes, with the sole intention of mating and laying more eggs, probably on your wood.

It will take many, many years for this small insect to devour the timber in a home completely, but it is disconcerting nevertheless.
Treatment Preservative fluids, as previously mentioned for the control of fungi attack, will invariably prevent damage due to the common furniture beetle. If however, an active attack is identified it is advisable to choose a solution which contains a contact insecticide. These are clearly marked by the manufacturer as also being a woodworm killer.

Application is as previously described but it must be remembered that the adult beetle can fly and it is a wise precaution to treat all wood in the vicinity of an attack.

Timber affected by woodworm

Chapter Ten

Paints, Preservatives and Protective Coatings

Correcting the damage caused by damp, decay and corrosion, can involve a great deal in terms of time, effort and money. Regular general maintenance and preservation will prove very worthwhile and avoid future expensive remedial work and replacement of material.

Paints and protective coatings enhance and prolong the life of property, keeping out damp, and so preventing deterioration of the building fabric.

When applying paints or similar materials, it must be stressed that preparatory work needs the utmost care, following the manufacturer's instructions at all times. The choice of materials is also important, and their use with the correct primer and undercoat is essential in order to gain the maximum life from any protective system.

Woodwork

For centuries wood has been used as a convenient building material. Especially today, with the very high cost of timber, it is important to protect it with every means at our disposal.

We have already seen that correcting dampness and decay in timber can involve a considerable amount of remedial work, but much can be done to protect and preserve the timber, thus preventing further expenditure.
Preservatives Almost all seasoned wood purchased today has been factory treated with a wood preservative; but as a precaution against rot and decay additional preservation is advisable, especially when the relatively low cost involved is considered.

Many varieties of preservatives are available, the most common and convenient for home application are those where the active ingredient is dissolved in a carrier solvent. These preservatives are easily applied by brush or spray and will not cause wood to warp or twist on drying.

Most manufacturers of preservatives produce a range of products, each grade being suited to a particular use. Careful selection of the grade used should be made, as some preservatives are designed for interior use and can be easily overpainted; others which

Individual knots should be treated with proprietary knotting before undercoating

are specially made for exterior use on property such as sheds and fences, contain a wood stain to produce their own attractive finish, and may not be suitable for overpainting.
Application Wood to be treated with preservative must be clean and free from any surface coatings such as paint, primers or knotting, all of which will prevent absorption of the preservative. Application, by brush or spray, is normally in two coats to enable the maximum penetration into the wood to be achieved. Areas of end grain and the joints of fabricated units must be given special attention to make sure they are saturated as thoroughly as is practical.
Painting For both exterior and interior woodwork, modern oil-based alkyd or polyurethane paints provide a durable coating. The use of eggshell or matt paint should be avoided, or at least limited to internal use on surfaces not exposed to possible abrasion – such as door surrounds. Varnishes are suitable for interior work, but for exterior ap-

plications rarely achieve the performance of a good quality gloss paint.

Procedure for New Wood New or stripped wood should be dry and thoroughly cleaned to remove all traces of dirt and grease. Surfaces should be rubbed down to a smooth finish and all dust removed. A thin coat of knotting should be applied to all knots; this will stop resin bleeding through the final paint film.

Prime hardwoods and non-resinous soft woods using a good quality wood primer; thinning the primer may help provide a good key for very hard, non-absorbent woods, such as oak or ash. An aluminium primer-sealer should be used on all resinous timbers such as Douglas Fir, Spruce and Pitch Pine.

Oily or greasy timbers similar to Afrormosia, Teak or Western Red Cedar, should also be primed with an aluminium sealer primer, after first washing down with white spirit to remove excess oil. If in doubt as to the correct priming system to use, always check with the paint manufacturer, or wood merchant for advice.

Once the primer has dried and hardened, all imperfections and open joints can be made good using a suitable wood filler.

One coat of the appropriate undercoat can then be applied. The final colour will be influenced by the undercoat and therefore, it is essential to use the appropriate undercoat to achieve the exact finish required. Two coats of gloss finish should be applied over the undercoat, using a fine sandpaper to lightly rub down between coats. Whenever possible, the undercoat and topcoats should be from the same manufacturer, to ensure that the highest degree of compatibility is obtained.

Previously Painted Wood Check existing paint films; if they are not in good condition the surface should be stripped and treated as new wood. Wash sound paint surfaces with a detergent or solvent to remove dirt and grease, and then rub down to a good surface with a fine sandpaper. Spot prime any areas of exposed wood, prior to applying the undercoat and two coats of gloss paint, rubbing down lightly between coats.

Timber already treated with many wood preservatives may simply be treated as new wood; some preservatives which stain the

Resin from untreated knot bleeding through, and discolouring paint film

timber, for example grades based on copper napthenate, will necessitate the timber being first primed with an aluminium sealer primer. This will prevent the colour of the preservative bleeding through the finishing coats. Other preservatives may prevent woodwork from receiving any paint film at all, and one should always check with the preservative manufacturer whether and how any specific grade can, if needed, be overpainted.

Metal Surfaces

Bare Metal Metal surfaces particularly iron and steel require protection to prevent corrosion in damp atmospheres. It is important to prepare surfaces thoroughly and to remove all corrosion products prior to the application of any protective coating. In industry this is normally done by pickling or shot blasting, but these methods are, of course, impossible for most home jobs.

The use of abrasives or wire brushing is not ideal, but if done carefully, and preferably by mechanical means, should produce an accept-

A high degree of protection can be afforded to wrought ironwork by application of a bitumen paint

able surface.

On bare iron and steelwork, a rust inhibitive primer must be used and applied immediately after completion of the preparatory work.

Quick-drying, red lead metal primers have good rust inhibitive qualities, but due to their lead content, are toxic. As an alternative, a chromate primer is less toxic, but its rust inhibitive function is slightly reduced.

Chromate primer should be used for all aluminium surfaces and its alloys, after first washing the surface with white spirit to remove any dirt and grease.

Galvanised surfaces, if new, will require the use of an etching or calcium plumbate primer. Galvanised surfaces which have weathered for several months, may accept treatment with a chromate metal primer.

Lead and copper surfaces may not require priming at all. Cleaning with white spirit to remove grease, and abrading lightly prior to application of the undercoat may be sufficient. Some manufacturers however do recommend the use of a 'chromate' priming system.

If in any doubts as to which priming system to use, or if an unusual surface is involved most paint manufacturers offer free advice as to the correct procedure to adopt.

Primed Metal Conventional oil-based paints should be applied to prepared metal in the manner as that described for wood, using one undercoat and two topcoats, and lightly rubbing down between coats. This will provide the most favourable protection, adhesion, maximum colour depth and a good high gloss surface.

In situations where a decorative appearance is not important, pure bitumen paint provides excellent protection over primed metal. Bitumen paints are black, and although glossy on application, rapidly take on a matt finish.

Used on gutters, down pipes, wrought ironwork or in cold water tanks, bitumen paints provide a very durable coating; it must be noted however, that conventional oil-based paints cannot be applied over bitumen, as the latter will bleed through.

As with all systems, the protection given by bitumen paints is proportional to the thickness of the film, and successive coats can be built up without the need to rub the surface down between coats. Subsequent applications are also simple; after removing any dirt or dust and correcting minor imperfections, extra coats can be easily applied without further preparatory work.

Previously Painted Metal Surfaces previously painted with conventional oil-based paints should be washed to remove dirt and grease and an abrasive paper used to provide a smooth surface. Any metal exposed should be spot primed as for bare metal, this primer being allowed to harden before continuing treatment as for primed surfaces, using one undercoat and two topcoats.

List of products and services

When tackling a task outlined in this publication, and for which task some materials will have to be purchased, the reader will usually find a wide range of brand names from which to choose.

The list given below therefore, is not definitive but will provide a choice of products of proven reliability, and if needed, sources for further information.

Adhesive – Flooring For sticking woodblocks, lino, etc, to concrete floors. Waterproof Bitumen. *Product:* Aquaprufe

Adhesive – Roofing Felt Bitumen. For sticking down roofing felt to concrete, etc., and chippings to roof surfaces. Also used as a lap-cement. *Product:* Aquaseal Firmafix

Dehumidifiers Remove excess moisture from air, providing a solution to condensation and dampness. *Product:* Haydon

Emulsions – Bitumen Waterproofing for roofs. *Product:* Aquaseal 5

Emulsion – Bitumen Heavy-Duty grade – recommended when ponding occurs on flat roofs. *Product:* Aquaseal 40

Fabric – Reinforcing For use as a reinforcing membrane in roof waterproofing treatments (with Aquaseal 5 and 40). *Product:* Aquaseal Fabric

Felts – Roofing Bitumen impregnated roofing felts all grades. *Product:* Aquaseal Roofing Felts

Finishes – Roof/Wall Coloured polymer waterproof finishes, red, green, grey, white for exterior surfaces of roofs and walls. *Product:* Aquaseal Coloured Finishes

Flashing Bitumen-backed aluminium (also lead coloured). Self adhesive. *Product:* Aquaseal Flashing

Insulants – Wall Thin, surface insulant sheeting for interior wall application. Helps maintain background heating and thus reduces condensation risks. *Product:* Kotina

Laminate – Damp Barrier Stops penetration of damp and efflorescent salts on to exterior surfaces of wall. *Product:* Aquaseal D.B. Kit (includes primer/adhesive)

Laths – Wall Provides a physical barrier to damp and a support for plaster/render. *Product:* Newtonite

Mastic Trowel-applied bitumen for sealing gaps, cracks in roofs and for gutter jointing. *Product:* Aquaseal 88

Membrane – Floors/Walls Bitumen-latex damp proof membrane for walls, floors, concrete beams and columns. *Product:* Aquaprufe

Paint – Aluminium Bitumen-based. For solar reflection on roofs and metal production. *Product:* Aquaseal A P

Paint – Bitumen Pure bitumen black paint for metal protections. Suitable for cold-water tank interior coating. *Product:* Aquaseal 44

Paint – Chlorinated Rubber For interior walls and ceilings damp-proof treatment. *Product:* Aquaseal 77

Polyurethane – Moisture Cured For surface-sealing very damp walls and floors. Ideal for basements, garages. Non-dusting. Resists physical damage. *Product:* Aquaseal Heavy Duty Urethane

Preservatives – Wood *Clear:* for all constructional timbers; may be painted, varnished or polished. *Green:* for garden and outdoor timber. *Brown:* Light or Dark; for all external timber. *Super:* all purposes; kills woodworm. *Red Cedar:* retains and restores the attractive appearance of Western Red Cedar. *Product:* Aquaseal Wood Preservatives

Repellents – Water For water-proofing most exterior building surfaces. Colourless. Contain silicones. *Product:* Aquaseal 66

Solvents – Bitumen Waterproofing for roofs especially suited for winter application, drying almost immediately on application. Standard, Super and Heavy-duty grades. *Product:* Aquaseal Weatherwise

Tape – Waterproofing Non-hardening base

fabric coated with waterproofing compound. For glazing bars, glass roofs, and general repairs. *Product:* Aquaseal Waterproofing Tape

Tiles – Roofing All types. *Product:* Marley

For further information and literature on these products and services, apply

Aquaseal/Aquaprufe
BP Aquaseal Limited
Kingsnorth, Hoo, Rochester, Kent ME3 9ND.
Tel: Medway (0634) 250722

Haydon Dehumidifiers
Hayden-Air Distribution Ltd
221 Old Christchurch Road, Bournemouth,
Dorset BH1 1PG.
Tel: Bournemouth (0202) 24592

Kotina
Metal Closures Rosslife Ltd
The Power House, Formby, Liverpool,
Lancashire.
Tel: Formby 72181

Marley Tiles
The Marley Roof Tile Co. Ltd
P.O. Box 19, Riverhead,
Sevenoaks, Kent TN13 2YU.
Tel: Sevenoaks (0732) 55255

Newtonite Lath
Newtonite Limited
166 Piccadilly, London W1V 0BX.
Tel: 01 409 0414

Phoenix Preservation Limited
Ilford, Essex.
Tel: 01 518 0921
(for timber treatment and damp proofing services)

Index

Acknowledgements

The authors wish to
acknowledge the valuable assistance given
in the preparation of the text of the book
by the following:

Gill Attwood
Technical Editor of the magazine
'Practical Householder'

Ken Nutt
Technical Sales Manager – BP Aquaseal Ltd

Carson Hadfields Ltd
Paint Manufacturers – Mitcham, Surrey

Andrew Sanders
Strawberry Hill Press Ltd., Twickenham

Graeme Withers
Design and illustrations